The Purpose of Suffering

Edwin Young

HARVEST HOUSE PUBLISHERS
Eugene, Oregon 97402

THE PURPOSE OF SUFFERING

Copyright © 1985 by Harvest House Publishers
Eugene, Oregon 97402

Library of Congress Catalog Card Number 85-80488
ISBN 0-89081-496-1

This book is gratefully dedicated to my mother, J. L. E. Young, and to the Second Baptist Church family. Individually, and corporately, both this godly woman and this body of Christ have exemplified for me what John had to say about the church in Philadelphia. Because of "a little power," keeping the Word, and not denying His name, God has blessed our church family, as He did my mother, with "an open door which no one can shut" (Revelation 3:8).

PREFACE

Volumes of counsel have been spoken and written on the subject of suffering and how we can survive our inevitable encounter with it. In a recent national poll, George Gallup discovered that the most frequently asked question in America is, "Why do people suffer?" The book of Job is God's answer.

One of the least-read books in the Bible, Job allows us a glimpse into the heavenlies to see a dimension we cannot comprehend. God's agenda is often totally different from what we expect. It is sometimes a frightening agenda. It is always a holy agenda!

Job, a righteous man, is afflicted with great pain and suffering. Three friends come to his side with one answer: "You are suffering because of sin. God is punishing you!"

Read Job and you will discover that this thesis is not true. God employs harsh words for these "friends" who lambaste Job with their false doctrine.

The advice of Job's friends, however, continues to echo throughout the land today. This "new doctrine" has become very, very popular. And why not? It states that as a child of God you can have complete health, wealth, and success just for the asking.

There are many sincere Christians who confidently "take cover" in the words of Mark 11:24:

> Therefore I tell you, whatever you ask for in prayer, believe that you have received it, and it will be yours.

This is one of the great promises of our Lord, but by taking this verse and others out of context, many people are led to false conclusions. The idea that almighty God is some kind of vending machine—"Name it and claim it!"—sounds great but is just not true.

God is sovereign. He is understood only in the total revelation of the Bible, and even then He cannot be completely understood by finite man. He works in our lives in ways we do not understand, and the Almighty does not ask our permission or offer an explanation. He is God! Read the total counsel of God and you will discover that the promises of God about answered prayer are conditional. An example of this principle is found in John 15:7: "Ask whatever you wish, and it will be given you."

Is this a blank check from God? Not at all. The first part of this verse states the condition of the promise: "*If* you remain in me and my words remain in you." Meet the conditions that precede the promise, and then the prayer of faith makes biblical sense!

"Name-it-and-claim-it" teaching simply does not consider the role of suffering within the whole context of Scripture. To exegete God's Word verse-by-verse is certainly enlightening, but to dissect Scripture with no thought of reassembling it is dangerous business. Principles derived from this kind of selective Bible study are questionable at best. For example, the thesis that all sickness and difficulty are the direct result of sin is just not biblical. Because of its very source and nature, sin is the *ultimate* cause of suffering, but this does not mean that every time a human being suffers he is being punished for a specific sin that he has committed.

In Isaiah 55:8,9 God clearly and succinctly relieves His children of the burden of "explaining" His holy and infinite ways:

"My thoughts are not your thoughts, neither are your ways my ways," declares the Lord. "As the heavens are higher than the earth, so are my ways higher than your ways and my thoughts than your thoughts."

When we genuinely accept our finite limits to understanding an infinite God, then we can begin to understand Job's character and his dilemma.

CONTENTS

1
Job's Megatrends

In the land of Uz there lived a man whose name was Job. This man was blameless and upright; he feared God and shunned evil.

He had seven sons and three daughters, and he owned seven thousand sheep, three thousand camels, five hundred yoke of oxen and five hundred donkeys, and had a large number of servants. He was the greatest man among all the people of the East.

His sons used to take turns holding feasts in their homes, and they would invite their three sisters to eat and drink with them.

When a period of feasting had run its course, Job would send and have them purified. Early in the morning he would sacrifice a burnt offering for each of them, thinking, "Perhaps my children have sinned and cursed God in their hearts." This was Job's regular custom.

One day the angels came to present themselves before the Lord, and Satan also came with them.

The Lord said to Satan, "Where have you come from?"

Satan answered the Lord, "From roaming through the earth and going back and forth in it."

Then the Lord said to Satan, "Have you considered my servant Job? There is no one on earth like him; he is blameless and upright, a man who fears God and shuns evil."

"Does Job fear God for nothing?" Satan replied. "Have you not put a hedge around him and his household and everything he has? You have blessed the work of his hands, so that his flocks and herds are spread throughout the land. But stretch out your hand and strike everything he has, and he will surely curse you to your face."

The Lord said to Satan, "Very well, then, everything he has is in your hands, but on the man himself do not lay a finger" (Job 1:1-12).

At this, Job got up and tore his robe and shaved his head. Then he fell to the ground in worship and said:

> *"Naked I came from my mother's womb,*
>   *and naked I will depart.*
> *The Lord gave and the Lord has taken away;*
>   *may the name of the Lord be praised."*

In all this, Job did not sin by charging God with wrongdoing (Job 1:20-22).

● ● ● ● ●

John Naisbitt's *Megatrends* is a book about the future. Based on meticulous research describing where America is today and where it will be tomorrow, the author analyzes 10 major trends that will shape our society and permeate every area of our lives. He points out that Americans were originally an agricultural people who developed into an industrial nation. Naisbitt states that our foundational structures have now changed, and that America's economy soon will be based primarily upon gathering and communicating information.

It is his projection that our gross national product and other previously reliable economic barometers will no longer be valid. We will be catapulted by powerful trends into new and unknown arenas. In 10 or 20 years many of us will be functioning in vocations we know nothing about today. Our lives will be changed—for some of us, *dramatically* changed. We face a new day that modern science has thrust upon us.

Change! Most of us resent it. We dislike the stress and pressure which accompany it. Some of us even try to deny that it is taking place. We long to go back to the "good old days." That, however, is an impossibility; change is here to stay! If your lifestyle has not yet experienced radical and dramatic change, just live a little longer...it will!

Consider Job, one of the world's greatest experts on stress! Perhaps no man in history ever suffered more tragedy or change or crisis than this ancient man.

Dr. P. D. O'Brien, a great Bible teacher, discovered all the major doctrines of our faith in the book of Job. Yet its 42 chapters are among the least understood passages in the Bible. To study Job is to study the oldest book in all the canon of Scripture. It was written in the time between Abraham and Moses, and therefore does not mention the Ten Commandments or the temple.

The Character of Job

The book begins with the biography of Job: "In the land of Uz there lived a man whose name was Job." Uz, in all probability, was located where modern Arabia is today. Scripture introduces Job as a godly man. First of all, the writer says that *he was a blameless man*. This word does not mean "perfect," as rendered in some translations. Rather, it means that he was "well-balanced." There were no rough edges on Job! He was a whole man with a complete personality. For example, if someone is honest, and yet lacks compassion, his Christian personality is not complete. God said about Job, "He is blameless." There was a wholeness about his life.

The description goes on to say that *he was upright*; he was straightforward. His word was always his bond. Job's handshake was safer than 12 pages drawn up by a Philadelphia lawyer! His contracts had no fine print!

In addition, Scripture describes him as a man who *feared God*. To be "God-fearing" as Job was doesn't mean that he was *frightened* of God or that he would run in fear from God. Instead, it implies a reverential attitude toward God. Job respected and was in awe of the Almighty. He understood clearly that God is holy. The fear of God, the Bible tells us, is the beginning of wisdom,

and the beginning of knowledge (Proverbs 1:7).
Job possessed both.

Job 1:1 continues by telling us that Job *shunned
evil*. When Job encountered evil, he would run for
his life. He did not play with sin, and he did not
give temptation a chance to entice him. Job could
discern evil because of his sensitive conscience and
spirit, and he would run from it. What a man! He
was blameless—upright—a man who feared God
and shunned evil. He seemed in every way to
personify righteousness.

Job's Treasures

Job was a *man of prosperity* (1:2,3). He was
blessed with children—seven boys and three girls.
He had a beautiful family! In addition, he was a
man of material wealth—7000 sheep, 3000 camels,
and 500 yoke of oxen. He would use two or
three oxen in every yoke, so he had at least a
thousand oxen. He also owned 500 donkeys and
several servants. Job was indeed a man of great
wealth.

Job also had a *marvelous relationship with his
family* (1:4,5). He would celebrate regularly with
his sons and daughters. They knew how to have
fun together; they knew how to laugh! There was
a cohesiveness in the family of Job—a much-
needed element in our society today.

The breakdown of relationships in the twentieth-
century home is a major problem. A mother
said to her 15-year-old daughter, "When I was
a teenager I didn't have the problems you have."

The daughter replied, "I know, Mom, but you

had better parents." Modern parents could learn much from Job!

Early in the morning, after the feasting and festivities were over, Job would gather his children and would privately and individually intercede for them before God. This intercession would involve his sacrificing a burnt offering for every child. Job, functioning as their priest, would *worship* with his children. A little phrase at the end of 1:5 indicates that he worshiped with regularity: "This was Job's regular custom."

Without a doubt, Job was the *greatest man in all the Eastern world* (1:3). Among the kings, satraps, princes, VIP's, and landowners, he was without peer.

Who can compete with this patriarch's credentials? He was a great man, a wealthy man, a prosperous man, an intelligent man! Job had enough sense to stay close to his family. As Luke wrote about another Child thousands of years later, we can say of Job's children that they "grew in wisdom and stature, and in favor with God and men" (2:52).

Parents so often say today, "I don't know what has happened to my son. Something must be wrong with his school or with our church. Why is he choosing wrong directions?"

What is wrong with that son? The home has the primary teaching responsibility in the life of a child. The primary place of worship for our children should also be the home. If parents neglect their responsibilities, what happens to a child in the church or in the school matters little. Almost without exception the home is the place where life's priorities are established and the direction of that young life determined.

Job developed a godly home by spending time with each of his children, by worshiping with them, and by interceding for them. He was burdened for each of them and was concerned that they might have cursed God secretly in their hearts (1:5b). He taught his children to be sensitive to both God and man.

Encounter in the Heavenlies

"One day the angels came to present themselves before the Lord, and Satan also came with them. The Lord said to Satan, 'Where have you come from?' Satan answered the Lord, 'From roaming through the earth and going back and forth in it' " (1:6,7).

In 1:7 the inspired writer permits us to look into "the heavenlies" (the name Paul gave to God's dwelling place). "The heavenlies" is what John saw while on the island of Patmos and recorded in the Revelation. He saw thousands and thousands of supernatural beings, angels and cherubim, together giving praise to God. The book of Job also pulls the curtain and allows us to observe what goes on in the council of God.

Job is written in both prose and poetry. It is primarily an epic poem, although the introduction and epilogue of the book are written in prose. These sections serve the same purpose as footnotes to a play. The book of Job is a true drama, with each character reciting a part of the epic poem while the prose footnotes explain the setting.

From the footnotes we see God on His throne, and the angels reporting to the Almighty. Satan enters into God's presence and speaks from the midst of the angelic beings.

Isaiah and Ezekiel tell us that Satan is nothing more than a fallen angel, filled with his own pride. Here in the presence of God he can observe first-hand God's activity. His reason for doing so is described in 1:6 by the use of one of Satan's names: *Apollyon*. This name means "The Destroying Angel," and explains his reason for coming into God's presence in the first place!

As the angels stand before God, the Lord Himself addresses Satan: "Satan, where have you been? What have you been doing?" (1:7a).

Satan's answer is classic: "I have been roaming to and fro on the earth" (1:7b).

What a perfect portrayal of the activity of evil and sin! Let sin come into your life, and you won't sleep; you will be restless; you will roam to and fro. Let sin come into your life, and you will be on edge; your temper will begin to express itself. Let sin come into your life, and everything will go wrong. You will blame everyone but yourself and your sin. Imagine Satan wandering up and down on the face of this earth, trying to find someone to deceive. This is a true picture of demonic activity!

One writer describes Satan as a cynic who hides among the angels in the throne room. With a sneer on his face he ridicules the other angels. Obviously, Satan is "turned off" by the activity in God's throne room.

Husbands who are dragged to church by their

wives sometimes give a similar impression. They look around and say, "It sure is boring here! Since I'm doing this for her, she'll have to make it up to me." The cynical expression of Satan is on their faces. They share something else with Satan: They squirm uncomfortably in sacred places!

God singled out Satan: "Satan, you've been going all over the earth trying to trick people. Have you looked at my man Job?" (1:8).

God describes Job with the same adjectives that are used at the beginning of chapter 1: "He is blameless and upright; he fears me, and he shuns evil" (1:8). Note the insidious response of Satan, the accuser. He begins with a question (1:9): "Does Job serve God for nothing? I've tried to get at him, but You have surrounded him with a hedge. Every time I try to attack at a weak point, or put pressure on his vanity, or try to hurt his family, his prosperity, or his personality—all the normal areas—You protect him."

Satan's Attack

Look at the deadly nature of Satan's accusation. If you lie about someone, you can be called into court. It is possible, however, to slander someone without making a blatant accusation. In 1:9-11 Satan directly attacks the motives of Job. Motives are difficult to defend. If a person says, "You stole my car," the one accused can reply, "No! I did not, and I can prove it." A defense can be developed against such an indictment. But if a person speculates, "The pastor is preaching so people will see him and make him feel important," he has

made an insinuation which is far more difficult
to defend. No one can really know the motives of
another person. Whether a deed is good or evil
often depends on the motive behind it. Satanic
attack stoops to question motives.

Satan subtly edges toward his victim: "Does Job
serve God for nothing?" He presumes that Job's
motives are selfish as he concludes: "God, if You
take away every possession he has, and if You
remove all his prosperity and prestige, he will curse
You to Your face!" (1:11).

The primary thesis of the story of Job is: *"Why
do the righteous suffer?"* A secondary and recur-
rent question is introduced by Satan himself:
"Why doesn't Job curse God?"

Job's generation believed that to curse God was
to die. In 1:5 Job expressed great fear that his
children, perhaps unknowingly, might have cursed
God in their hearts. Satan, in contrast, would
have been delighted to hear Job curse God to His
face! Confident that this would not happen, God
pointed out Job to Satan. It was God Himself who
challenged Satan's cynicism about the motives of
Job.

If Satan could question Job's motives, and even
question God's motives for blessing Job, we
should feel free to question *Satan's* motives in our
own lives. From his hidden agenda, Satan was
trying to establish his superiority over Job: "If
You only knew his true motives, You would see
that he is not as good or deserving as I am." If
Satan could have proved that point, he would have
boasted to all the beings of the universe that
goodness does not exist.

Because Satan sees goodness as simply a state of mind, he seeks to blot it out with an alternate agenda of hate and garbage, destruction and immorality, inconsistency and dishonesty. Even as he did this, Satan contradicted his own premise: "At least I'm no hypocrite; I'm *honest* about my motives!"

So many of Satan's children use the same logic. They think it is all right to be devious and corrupt, *as long as they're not hypocritical about it*. They point to those who go to church and say, "Well, I may do this and that, but at least I don't go to church and pretend to be pious like those hypocrites do!" That logic is totally untenable— unless you think the way Satan thinks.

A man who once claimed to be a God-fearing churchman divorced his wife and is now living with a young woman in open adultery. He is very candid about his new lifestyle when he comments, "At least I'm *honest* about it." It's almost as if being open about evil justified it before God. That is twisted logic indeed!

Suppose a man walks into a small town and robs the bank. He enters the bank, draws a gun, and says, "Hand over your money." The tellers hand over the cash. The man casually puts the money into a bag, puts the gun in his pocket, and walks nonchalantly down the street. A few blocks away the police catch him. Because he has been open and honest, and has not tried to run away, will he escape punishment for his crime? Of course not! Even so, impure actions are not "purified" by a person's openness about them.

Clearly, a person has no merit for either hiding

or displaying the garbage of his or her lifestyle. In both cases, the only viable solution is to dispose of it. Garbage, after all, is to be thrown away!

If asked to summarize the story of Job, someone might say that God and Satan are in a battle, and that Job is caught in the middle. This summation reveals a grave misunderstanding many people today have about Satan. He is often spoken of as having the same attributes of and equality with God. This is just not true. There is not one good God and another evil god in the universe. Satan is a limited, created, fallen being whose end is described in Revelation. He will be confined to this earth; later he will be thrown into the bottomless pit, bound for a thousand years. There will then be a brief revolution by evil men—an attempted coup d'etat against the Lord Jesus Christ. Following this final uprising, Satan will be sentenced to the eternal pit of fire. He is not equal with God!

In his attack on Job (1:13ff.), Satan took full advantage of the limits God had given him. In Job's first test, God limited Satan by saying, "You can do anything else to him, Satan, but don't touch his body!" Within those bounds Satan pushed his victim to the edge.

First came reports from messengers who said, "Job, marauders from the north came and took away all your donkeys. They have stolen all your oxen and murdered all your servants who were watching after them." Then another messenger arrived, saying, "Oh, Job! Lightning came down and struck all your sheep. They are all dead."

Still another messenger arrived, saying, "Job,

your camels have been taken away by the Chaldeans!'' Another messenger reported, "Oh, Job! I don't know how to break the news to you. *All* of your children—your seven sons and your three daughters—*all* were in the house of their older brother, and a tornado tore the roof away. It collapsed on them, and all are dead.''

Calamity happened in such swift strokes— our tragic events caused by the great destroyer, Apollyon! Note how the text ties the impact of one report to the next with the phrase "while he was yet saying." "While he was yet saying"...the camels! "While he was yet saying"...the sheep! "While he was yet saying"...the servants! Each tragedy crashed into the next until the consummate blow was delivered—*"all your children!"*

Kept by God

Be certain of this fact: Satan *never* has ultimate control of the wind and the rain, and the agenda of this world. At times God in His permissive will may allow Satan to control the elements temporarily, but even then God puts a hedge around such permitted activity. If Satan were free to run this world without limits, he would bring us all to a quick and tragic end. Ultimately, God is in charge. We do not always understand why God gives Satan even temporary permission to control situations, or why Satan would be allowed to control the elements of our environment. It is hard to grasp why he is allowed to work through people and nations, causing them to attack and to steal, to incite pain and destruction. However, we can be utterly confident that through it all, and unknown to Satan, God can and will use every crisis for His own glory and for man's good.

What did Satan predict Job would do when God allowed all his blessings to be removed? "God, he'll curse You to Your face!" (1:11).

The first thing Job did was to shave his head and tear his clothes—an Oriental sign of mourning. Job was no stoic. He did not deny his great loss. In a very human way he acknowledged that the bottom had fallen out of his life. He could not touch solid ground. He did exactly what any person would do: He wept uncontrollably.

What did he do then? He went to the "first cause."

Job knew that the first cause of everything is *God*. He did not blame the Chaldeans or the Sabeans; he did not blame the wind or the rain; he did not blame chance or the capricious "lady luck" of the pagan world. He didn't even blame Satan. He didn't blame anybody or anything. *He went to God!* He did not come before God to rebuke Him. He didn't even ask Him a question, as he would later on.

The book of Job is primarily about one supreme, anguished question that begins with *"Why?"* The "Why?" is always more powerful than the "Where?" the "How?" or the "When?" The tough question always begins with "Why?"

Job repeatedly asked "Why?" as he was engulfed in a sea of trouble, but he did not do so with this first test. Instead he said, "I came into this world naked. I'll leave this world naked. The Lord gives and the Lord takes away." He was saying, "God, I thank You for providing my possessions while I had them. I thank You for my prestige and my position when they existed. I thank You for every moment I had with my children. How beautiful, how precious, how sweet they were! O Lord, I thank You for all of this. Lord God, You gave it all to me. Now, in Your divine will, You have taken it all away." Did he then say, "Cursed be God"? No. Instead he said, "Praised be the name of the Lord!" In his first test, Job came through the tragedy triumphantly.

My grandfather had a country store. Sometimes he would be paid with counterfeit coins. He would strike every coin on the counter and listen to the ring of the metal in it. Unless he heard a certain sound, he would not accept the money.

God allowed Satan to treat Job as though he were a coin, and to strike him on the counter of life. God knew that the gold in this man's heart would ring true and could be deposited in the heavenly treasury! Satan would discover in Job the quality and genuineness of a man of God. As a result of the testing he endured, Job understood more about himself and his God than he could have learned under any other circumstances.

God is the master metallurgist who will always care for His own as precious gold. When He does allow the fire of suffering, it is only for the purpose and privilege of refinement. Only the real stuff—that which is pure—survives. All the dross, all the unnecessary will be burned away. In His great plan God will take us out of the fire of suffering and privation and return us to life as refined gold. Only then will we begin to effectively serve the purpose for which we were created: to have an intimate relationship with God and to honor and glorify Him with all that we are.

When C.S. Lewis was asked "Why do the righteous suffer?" his answer was "Why not? They are the only persons who can handle it." Paul summed it up when he wrote, "We know that in all things God works for the good of those who love him, who have been called according to his purpose" (Romans 8:28). If we could see as God sees, we would know that everything which happens to us is ultimately for our good and for His glory.

Chapter Insights

1. Uprightness of character does not prevent suffering in the Christian life.
2. God's agenda for our lives revolves around faithfulness, not understanding.
3. It is not necessary to know *how* an affliction will be remedied in order to have faith that it *will* be.

2
The Rules Change

On another day the angels came to present themselves before the Lord, and Satan also came with them to present himself before him.

And the Lord said to Satan, "Where have you come from?"

Satan answered the Lord, "From roaming through the earth and going back and forth in it."

Then the Lord said to Satan, "Have you considered my servant Job? There is no one on earth like him; he is blameless and upright, a man who fears God and shuns evil. And he still maintains his integrity, though you incited me against him to ruin him without any reason."

"Skin for skin!" Satan replied. "A man will give all he has for his own life. But stretch out your hand and strike his flesh and bones, and he will surely curse you to your face."

The Lord said to Satan, "Very well, then, he is in your hands; but you must spare his life."

So Satan went out from the presence of the Lord

and afflicted Job with painful sores from the soles of his feet to the top of his head. Then Job took a piece of broken pottery and scraped himself with it as he sat among the ashes.

His wife said to him, "Are you still holding on to your integrity? Curse God and die!"

He replied, "You are talking like a foolish woman. Shall we accept good from God, and not trouble?"

In all this, Job did not sin in what he said (Job 2:1-10).

● ● ● ● ●

The book of Job is one of the greatest books in all the literature of mankind. Thomas Carlisle said, "There is nothing like Job in the Bible or outside the Bible for literary excellence alone."

Undoubtedly, the story of Job was presented first in dramatic form, with all the characters acting to transmit its message to vast audiences of the ancient world. As they watched, they listened carefully to the fundamental truths being hammered out on the anvil of Job's life.

The story of Job is not written in the abstract. It begins with a person: "There was a man named Job." Its subject is not theory and philosophy, but a flesh-and-blood man who finds himself in the middle of his own sea of trouble. Time and time again Job asks "Why?" His friends and remaining family echo the unfathomable lament: "Why? Why?"

The Agony of "Why?"

"Why?" is a familiar question to us all. "Why did that happen? Why that tragedy? Why that event?" So much is inexplicable. I do not understand so many of the "why's" of life. Job asks the toughest "Why?" of all: "Why do good people suffer?"

We know why wicked people suffer: "Do not be deceived: God cannot be mocked. A man reaps what he sows. The one who sows to please his sinful nature, from that nature will reap destruction; the one who sows to please the Spirit, from the Spirit will reap eternal life" (Galatians 6:7,8). That's the law of the harvest! Whatever you sow, that is also what you reap. In Job's day all the people agreed (as many believe today) that a man's spiritual stability and his relationship to God are reflected by his station in life. If trouble touches someone, and it seems to be compounded semiannually, people wonder, "What sin has he committed?"

Another person sees everything within reach turn to gold. Then people say, "Ah, he has special favor with God."

We have seen that after Job's possessions and his family were taken from him, he does not curse God, as Satan had predicted. Instead, he praises the Lord: "The Lord gave and the Lord has taken away; may the name of the Lord be praised" (1:21b).

With that commited word of praise, Job makes a definite statement about the sovereignty of God: He is in charge of everything that is, and everything that will be...forever. Job does not see what is going on in the heavenlies between Satan and God. Job does not know that he is God's example of a man of great faith. Certainly if Job had known more, he would have been more tolerant of the unhappy events in his life. Then his foot would have been upon Satan's neck! When tragedy touches us, we, like Job, usually do not fully understand what is taking place. When prosperity or calamity comes, we either exult or shatter into tiny pieces—all without the full picture of what is happening to us. We do not comprehend events that are so often beyond our control. Job is saying to us, "If you could only see and know what God is doing in this world and through your life, you would understand."

Chapter 2 elaborates on the details of Job's suffering. Once again God assembles the angelic creatures before Him, and we see Satan walking around in their presence. God summons Satan and says, "Satan, where have you been?" Again he gives the hedgy answer, "Going to and fro. Walking up and down." Then God mentions Job.

It is good that Job did not know anything about this conversation. He might have said, "God, please don't talk about me! I've been through enough."

From this side of Calvary, we know a truth that Job could not know, although it was operating in his life: "No temptation has overtaken you but such as is common to man; and God is faithful, who will not allow you to be tempted beyond what you are able, but with the temptation will provide the way of escape also, that you may be able to endure it" (1 Corinthians 10:13 NASB). We will not be tested beyond our capacity to endure, for God has prepared us! We will not face suffering, or know privation and pressure, which God will not enable us to withstand victoriously.

Then Satan sarcastically challenges the Lord: "The score at the end of the first inning is Job, one, Satan, nothing. But we have only started, God. Now I have a request: skin for skin."

What is Satan saying? He is claiming that even though an individual could survive the loss of loved ones or a financial rating, he would still have a hard time losing his own health. So Satan requests, "Let me touch Job's body. Then surely he will curse You to Your face!"

Remember the principle: "Gold is never destroyed by fire—only refined." God responds by moving His previously set boundaries and Satan is granted access to Job's physical health. But God stipulates, "You must spare his life" (Job 2:6).

Three-Pronged Attack of Satan

Satan immediately begins a three-pronged attack. Job is attacked physically, emotionally, and spiritually. The spiritual battle fills most of the book from Job 2:10 until the final words of chapter 42.

The physical attack is horrendous. Satan afflicts Job with boils—literally "fiery boils"—from the crown of his head to the bottom of his feet. His whole body is covered with boils. Many commentators believe that he had a deadly form of leprosy; or perhaps he had elephantiasis, a disease with more terrible symptoms than pus-filled boils.

Such a disease would cause the face and feet to swell out of proportion, and the hands and nose to grow unusually large. The skin reddens and develops the pitted texture of an elephant's hide. Job's whole countenance was gaunt and distorted because of the infection and burning pain. We see a picture of Job scraping himself with broken pieces of pottery because of the constant itching. His speech is affected by the disease; his words have a hollow, nasal quality. What a wreck of a man!

Whenever Satan is allowed access to a life, that person is in trouble! We need to thank God that He keeps His children in the palm of His hand and never allows a hair on our heads to be touched without His permission. But here in His sovereignty God uses Satan's attack to teach and to demonstrate. Suddenly Job is the most miserable of men. Months pass. The Bible pictures him sitting among the ashes as a penniless pauper, stripped of all his possessions and children, and afflicted with disease. "He took a piece of broken pottery and scraped himself" (2:8).

Next, Satan attacks Job emotionally. His wife enters the scene and offers two devastating words of counsel to her husband: "The best thing you can do is curse God and die." In the very same breath she urges her husband to blaspheme God and to commit suicide. She becomes the first biblical advocate of mercy killing! Then she adds to his pain with the cutting question in 2:9: "Do you still claim to be a man of integrity?"

While Job seems to be dying, his wife has a field

day! Instead of building up her husband, she taunts him with innuendoes. His health is gone, and now his emotional support is withdrawn when he needs it most. Job is totally alone.

Do wives really understand how important their emotional support is to their husbands? Every successful husband needs that special helpmate who gives support and encouragement as only a wife can. So often the real test of love and fidelity comes during those especially difficult times.

After Job loses his health and his emotional support, he is particularly vulnerable to Satan's spiritual attack. His three friends—Eliphaz, Bildad, and Zophar—are very important tools in the hands of Satan. These men come from different parts of the country and play significant roles in the bombardment of Job. Among his peers, Job enjoys a reputation as the greatest man in the East. When they hear about his plight, they cannot believe it, and so they come to see for themselves. But Job is so grotesquely distorted that they don't even recognize him! They weep when they see Job's condition, tearing their clothes to symbolize their mourning with him. They then sit on the ground with the patriarch for seven days and seven nights, remaining silent because of his great suffering.

What should we do to help someone in a time of crisis? How should we act when something happens in the life of a friend, or when we go into a home where tragedy has come? When we do not know what to say or do, sometimes the best thing to say is...nothing! Just to sit down and cry with a friend is to say "I care."

When Susie came home from school, her mother could tell that something was wrong. "What happened today?" she asked.

"Oh, just the usual." Susie paused. Then, in a pensive tone, she continued, "Margie came back today. Her father died last week."

"What did you say to her?"

"Well, I didn't know what to say...so I just sat by her, and we cried together."

The Bible tells us that Job's friends sat with him for seven days, the length of a funeral ritual in that culture. Actually, Job is watching his friends as they enact the mourning ritual of his funeral service. During this time they mourn and agonize in silence over the imminent death of their friend.

While Job's friends are consoling him, they are composing the speeches that are found in the remaining chapters. At first they are horrified at the sight of Job in his condition. They readily empathize with him in tears and anguish. He is their brother, their friend, and their companion. Finally it hits them: "For all this to have happened—for Job to have lost all that he had so suddenly, and then to be dying as well—surely Job is a terrible sinner."

When we read between the lines, we see that the friends' comments seem to evolve from pure grief to a curious skepticism. The "why" creeps back in. They become hard, cold, and judgmental. In their pious diagnosis they determine, "What a terrible, despicable, immoral person you are, Job. We've never seen anybody in such a condition before! What did you do to bring all this upon yourself?" With this assessment, his friends turn away. They begin to assault him spiritually by attacking his beliefs, his theology, and even his personal walk with God. Job has been bombarded physically and emotionally, and now the spiritual guns are leveled at him. Satan does his utmost to shoot down Job's faith in God! He is determined to force Job to curse God and die.

Integrity and Faith Maintained

In the face of this three-pronged offensive, Job maintains two things. First of all, he maintains his integrity. He never confesses to something he did not do. He never claims to be guilty of a great sin that would give a reason for his dilemma. He always maintains that he walked before the Lord in a straightforward manner.

In the second place, Job never forfeits his belief in God. Consider the ammunition used against him: all the theology of that patriarchal period! His situation was sized up in light of every conceivable theological argument. Yet as Job endures pain and rejection night after night and day after day, he adamantly maintains, "I still trust in my God!"

The rules have been changed, and the limits have been moved to allow Satan to intensify his attack on Job's person, but still Job remains unshakable in his confidence that God will give meaning to it all. Such a quality of faith is needed so desperately in our generation! If we are called to live the life that goes to the depths of pain and anguish, we need to pray for faith that will eliminate our doubt and give sense and sanity to the meaningless, unknown places. We must never lose our integrity or waver in our faith and confidence in God. Then we can cope with whatever problems we encounter in this life.

Since everyone either *has* a problem, *is* a problem, or *lives with* a problem, it is vitally important that we never lose our integrity or waver in our faith and confidence in God. It is this very kind of faith that will allow us to cope with whatever problems we encounter in this life.

Chapter Insights

1. Satan always attacks at our precise points of weakness.
2. Satan uses people who are close or important to us to gain access to those vulnerable spots in our lives.
3. Job seemed to realize that he was not responsible for what other people thought of him, but was responsible for remaining faithful to God's plan for his life.
4. As circumstances worsened, Job's faith and integrity became a necessity for his survival!

3

The Impatience of Job

After this, Job opened his mouth and cursed the day of his birth. He said:

"May the day of my birth perish, and the night it was said, 'A boy is born!' That day—may it turn to darkness; may God above not care about it; may no light shine upon it. May darkness and deep shadow claim it once more; may a cloud settle over it; may blackness overwhelm its light. That night— may thick darkness seize it; may it not be included among the days of the year nor be entered in any of the months. May that night be barren; may no shout of joy be heard in it. May those who curse days curse that day, those who are ready to rouse Leviathan. May its morning stars become dark; may it wait for daylight in vain and not see the first rays of dawn, for it did not shut the doors of the womb on me to hide trouble from my eyes.

"Why did I not perish at birth, and die as I came from the womb? Why were there knees to receive me and breasts that I might be nursed? For now

*I would be lying down in peace; I would be asleep
and at rest with kings and counselors of the earth,
who built for themselves places now lying in ruins,
with rulers who had gold, who filled their houses
with silver.*

*Or why was I not hidden in the ground like a
stillborn child, like an infant who never saw the
light of day? There the wicked cease from turmoil,
and there the weary are at rest. Captives also enjoy
their ease; they no longer hear the slave driver's
shout. The small and the great are there, and the
slave is freed from his master.*

*"Why is light given to those in misery, and life
to the bitter of soul, to those who long for death
that does not come, who search for it more than
for hidden treasure, who are filled with gladness
and rejoice when they reach the grave? Why is life
given to a man whose way is hidden, whom God
has hedged in? For sighing comes to me instead
of food; my groans pour out like water. What I
feared has come upon me; what I dreaded has
happened to me. I have no peace, no quietness;
I have no rest, but only turmoil"* (Job 3:1-26).

Then Eliphaz the Temanite replied:

*"If someone ventures a word with you, will you
be impatient? But who can keep from speaking?
Think how you have instructed many, how you
have strengthened feeble hands. Your words have
supported those who stumbled; you have strengthened faltering knees. But now trouble comes to
you, and you are discouraged; it strikes you, and
you are dismayed"* (Job 4:1-5).

*Consider now: Who, being innocent, has ever
perished? Where were the upright ever destroyed?*

As I have observed, those who plow evil and those who sow trouble reap it. At the breath of God they are destroyed; at the blast of his anger they perish. The lions may roar and growl, yet the teeth of the great lions are broken. The lion perishes for lack of prey, and the cubs of the lioness are scattered (Job 4:7-11).

• • • • •

Job's friends sit with him for seven days and seven nights, in total silence, because of his terrible pain. Until this point in his tragedy, Job's attitude has been, "The Lord gave; the Lord has taken away. I just praise the name of my God." What a great man! In his word to Ezekiel, the Lord called Job righteous. Is it any wonder Ezekiel said that Job was one of the three great men in the Bible (Ezekiel 14:14)? By every human standard, Job was a patient man.

Job 3 is a transitional chapter. As it begins, evidently Job has been sick a long time. The days have turned into months, and perhaps years have passed. The anguish continues. As far as Job is concerned, the heavens have turned to brass. Surely God has forgotten him! In desperation, Job asks three devastating questions of God.

The Resignation of Job

The first question he asks is recorded in verses 2 through 10 of the third chapter. "Why didn't I die when I was born?" Job curses the day of his birth. He remarks, "When you remember my

birthday, paint that day black on your calendar.
I don't want anyone to know a man named Job
ever lived. There is no blessing involved in my
birth."

His second question is in verses 11 through 19:
"Lord, if I had to live through my birth, why
didn't I die soon afterward? Why didn't I die as
a baby?" He tells God he could have fallen out
of his mother's lap. She could have fed him
improperly. Disease could have killed him.

In verses 20 through 26, the third devastating
question is asked. Job asks, "Lord, if You would
not let me die when I was a baby, why can't You
let me die right this minute? I am ready to go!
What possible good can be done by a man like me,
covered with boils, feverish and in pain, scraping
these sores, embarrassed, penniless? Just kill me,
God. I'm ready to die!"

We all know people who have prayed like that.
I think of Uncle Jimmy Smathers, who was in his
late nineties and lived in the Great Smoky Moun-
tains. When a friend of mine visited him, Uncle
Jimmy looked at him and said, "Young man, I've
been praying that I would die. All my family is
gone. All my friends are gone. I've outlived every-
body, and I know the Lord. I just want to die.
Why won't God let me die?"

Like Uncle Jimmy, Job is ready to die! He
rationalizes, "I'm fed up with life, and everything
is coming up zeros for me. There is no purpose
in living anymore." In this mood, he not only
questions his reasons for living, but he also questions the very essence of God: His character and
even His love.

The Rationalization of Eliphaz

In chapter 4 the first of Job's friends speaks. I call him Eliphaz the Eloquent because he was some kind of orator! Evidently he was the oldest of the friends, since he spoke before the others. Eliphaz's verbiage is as smooth and slick as boiled okra. He says, "I would like to have a word. Job, practice what you preach. You have been so skilled in counseling others who have been sick and who have had problems and difficulties. You have been able to help them work through the vicissitudes of their lives. Now, Job, it's your turn. You have talked a good talk, but you have not put your advice to work in your own life. Practice what you preach!"

Then Eliphaz offers his explanation for Job's suffering (4:7-11). His philosophy, by the way, is still held by many people today: "Job, have you ever known a good man to suffer the way you're suffering? Can you name even *one*?"

Many of us would say, "I never think that way," and yet we really do! When we hear of some calamity taking place, we immediately conclude that someone is being punished for something. Suppose a news bulletin announced that Moscow had been struck by an earthquake. Some would say immediately, "God is dealing with Moscow!"

Years ago, the editor of a particular magazine alleged in an article that Billy Graham was ill because he had associated with the wrong kind of people. In the next month's edition, it was reported that the editor had fallen down a flight of

stairs and broken his leg. The editor explained that
Satan was attacking his God-given ministry! If
something bad happens to you, I may assume that
the judgment of God is upon your sin. But if
something bad happens to me, I will have another
rationale altogether!

Eliphaz says to Job, "You are a hypocrite, a
liar, and a fraud. I've suspected it all the time.
Now finally you're getting what you deserve. Why
don't you practice what you preach? You have
told everyone else what to do, but now that trouble
has come to you, you are impatient!"

Eliphaz tells Job that he is, of all things, an
impatient man (4:5). Does that surprise you? If
you were being quizzed about Bible characters,
how would you answer the question "Who was
the most patient man?" Why, Job, of course!

Contrary to this popular belief, we see in chapter
3 an *impatient* Job cursing the day of his birth.
Why was he born? Why did he not die during his
childhood? Now his strength and energy are gone,
his endurance dissipated. He is at the end of his
rope! And Eliphaz's counsel only makes matters
worse. Job cries, "Oh that my request might come
to pass, and that God would grant my longing!
Would that God were willing to crush me!" (6:8,9
NASB).

The Practicality of Patience

Some time ago our minister of music had an
impacted tooth and was in excruciating pain
during our first morning worship service. He even
had to have his tooth drilled just to get through

the second service. It might have seemed that I had tremendous patience with his pain, but in fact I was really indifferent to it; I didn't even know about it until later in the day. We often confuse patience with indifference. When we are truly *patient* with others we are exercising the power to wait for a hoped-for good. That is patience.

Patience is the power to wait for a hoped-for good, even when that good is your husband, who is late for dinner and all the food is cold.

It is the power to wait for a hoped-for good when that good is your wife, who is never on time for anything!

Patience is the power to wait for that hoped-for good when your teenage daughter has been lying on the floor with her feet up in the air and her hand clutching the telephone for endless hours.

Patience is the power to wait for that hoped-for good while your teenage son is making his way up fool's hill.

Patience is the power to wait for that hoped-for good when the order you placed in a restaurant has not arrived 45 minutes later. Patience is the power to wait for the end of a sermon you thought would go on forever!

Patience is all these things . . . and much, much more!

The Requisities of Patience

Just exactly how does a person acquire patience? In the first place, we must realize that patience is a child of desire. You must want to cultivate patience. Hebrews 12:1 tells us to run the race (life itself) that is set before us, and to run it with patience. In Galatians 5:22,23 Paul talks about the fruit in the garden of your heart that is cultivated and nurtured by the Holy Spirit. That fruit of the Spirit includes love, joy, peace, and...patience! We have to *desire* patience for it to become a viable part of our character and to have an impact on our everyday living.

Also, patience is a child of faith. Thomas Edison was a brilliant and gifted scientist, but without his persevering patience we might be still in the dark, or still reading by candlelight. In contrast, we have all encountered uncommonly gifted individuals who lack patience. They have everything going for them in terms of gray matter and external resources, but they never quite get off the ground. So often they quit too soon; they don't press on. This is not the patience that Paul mentioned in Philippians 3:14: "I press on toward the goal for the prize of the upward call of God in Christ Jesus" (NASB).

Patience is also a child of love. Just as surely as God is loving, He is supremely patient. Look how long it took God's children to comprehend His basic command: "Thou shalt have no other gods before me" (Exodus 20:3 KJV).

God was loving and patient over hundreds of years. How long did it take for God's children to understand and comply with His marriage plan of one husband and one wife? Again, hundreds of years.

The Patience of God

We know a God who waits and loves at the same

time, who never takes a shortcut or uses a round-about method to accomplish His will for His own. He never gives up on us; He keeps on loving, reaching, and believing in us. As almighty and powerful as He is, still He waits.

In His omnipotence, God knows what we really need far better than we do! He answered that need in the incarnation of Christ. Patiently, God became a man and dwelt among us so that we could better understand the depth of His infinite love. He didn't come as a prince; He came as a peasant. He didn't come as a conqueror; He came as a carpenter. That same carpenter rode into the city of Jerusalem on the back of a donkey! We call that ride His "triumphal entry." What a paradox! It was *the patience of God* which triumphed that day. Jesus could have had the universe at His feet or legions of angels for His protection. Yet He rode into the city that was to be the site of His execution. Who can really understand such humility and patience, born only from supernatural love?

If only because of his historical perspective, Job deserves a compassionate look from us on this side of Calvary. As we walk though suffering, we can begin to understand the principle that has not yet been made evident for Job: "My grace is sufficient for you, for my power is made perfect in weakness" (2 Corinthians 12:9).

Chapter Insights

1. When we lose confidence in God, there is no

remaining basis for confidence in self. Resignation signals the death of faith. Giving up on life leads to an early grave!

2. When a person rationalizes, he mistakes his own subjective viewpoint for an objective and unbiased one.

3. The *practice* of patience is the only means of *developing* patience.

4

What Are Friends For?

A despairing man should have the devotion of his friends, even though he forsakes the fear of the Almighty. But my brothers are as undependable as intermittent streams, as the streams that overflow when darkened by thawing ice and swollen with melting snow, but that cease to flow in the dry season, and in the heat vanish from their channels. Caravans turn aside from their routes; they go up into the wasteland and perish. The caravans of Tema look for water, the traveling merchants of Sheba look in hope. They are distressed, because they had been confident; they arrive there, only to be disappointed. Now you too have proved to be of no help; you see something dreadful and are afraid. Have I ever said, "Give something on my behalf, pay a ransom for me from your wealth, deliver me from the hand of the enemy, ransom me from the clutches of the ruthless"? Teach me, and I will be quiet; show me where I have been wrong (Job 6:14-24).

• • • • •

In 1983, Hurricane Alicia struck the city of Houston with tornadoes and torrential rains. Great numbers of people were without water and electrical power for days. Devastating winds ripped the roofs from many houses. Uprooted trees lay everywhere.

In the aftermath of that storm, I made an amazing discovery. If I had been asked to select the trees in my neighborhood that would withstand the storm, I would have picked the two huge oak trees that command the attention of every person driving down my street. Surely the skinny little pines would have blown over, but I would have guaranteed that those oaks would stand! Curiously, those two oaks were the first trees to go!

After the storm, I watched tree surgeons with truck and cranes and bulldozers as they pulled up the remaining roots. Finally I asked one of the men, "What happened to these oak trees? Of all the trees, they were the most powerful ones. Why did they fall?"

The tree expert replied, "Look at the roots. On one of the oaks, the roots are rotten. On the other tree, the trunk is hollow. Bore worms have destroyed it." Both of these trees had looked perfectly healthy before the storm came. The foliage, the branches, and the bark gave the appearance of tremendous trees! Problems began, however, when the pressure of the wind came: One lacked strong roots, and the core of the other was hollow and rotten. Neither tree could stand the strong winds!

Could Job have been like these trees? He looked so fine on the outside. He was a man of God and a man of prayer. He enjoyed prestige and prosperity, a wonderful family and caring friends. Yet in a brief period Job lost everything. Did he curse the day he was born and beg God to take his life because of sin in his life? Was he infected with boils to the point of complete exhaustion because of a secret, deliberate transgression?

Job's three friends, Eliphaz the Eloquent, Bildad the Blaster, and Zophar the Zealous, continue to make their presumptuous and senseless speeches to the suffering patriarch. Eliphaz the Eloquent, that long-winded orator, accuses him of being impatient.

We need a calendar instead of a clock to time Eliphaz's oration! With all his confidence, Eliphaz drones on and on. Tediously he builds his case against Job. Now and then Eliphaz's words sting Job a little, but generally he uses worn platitudes.

Friends Without Discernment

In his eloquent way Job states, "My friends have let me down." Has a friend ever disappointed you? Has a good friend ever let you down? You were confident that he or she would help, but when the crisis came and the need was expressed, that friend just was not available.

Job's friends came to him physically, but they let him down emotionally. He said, "They do not show pity." The Hebrew word is *chesed*. The word is translated in our Bibles as *kindness* or *loving-kindness*. Job said, "I need pity from my friends.

I need sympathy and empathy and understanding. I need lovingkindness.''

There is a difference between *kindness* and *lovingkindness*. When your son comes home from school and says, ''Mom, make me a jelly sandwich,'' and you take a piece of bread and put jelly on it, that is kindness. If you take a piece of bread and put jelly *and butter* on the sandwich, that is *lovingkindness*!

Kindness or lovingkindness. . . . Job would have settled for either one! Even though they failed their friend in his time of distress, they at least came to him.

The great tragedy is that some of us don't do even as well as Job's friends! We are not discerning enough to know when friends need us and when we should be available.

Can you imagine the trial of the robber who had attacked the man on the Jericho road and left him for dead? Can you imagine the testimony of the priest and Levite if they were called to the witness stand?

''Did you see the man who was robbed and beaten?'' the prosecuting attorney asks the Levite.

Answer: ''Yes, I saw him, but I thought he might be pretending. Maybe he was a robber. I was afraid! Anyway, I was in a hurry. I really didn't see him very well because I passed on the other side.''

Then the priest takes the stand. Question: ''Well, what did you see?''

Answer: ''I looked at him and rolled him over, but I thought he was a dead man. Besides, I was already late for an appointment. There was no need for me to get involved. Someone would find him later. Anyway, he looked dead to me!''

Most of us respond to need in these very same ways! Even though we see it, we do not understand or comprehend it. People constantly say to me, ''I am so burdened about this person who does not know the Lord Jesus Christ. Please go and visit him.'' Instead of using an established relationship as a base, we try to reach that person through a total stranger.

If someone is on your heart, *you* go to him! We are afraid to have friends because it costs something to be a friend. People whom we thought were our friends have hurt us so we are reluctant to give ourselves again. We do not take the risk because being vulnerable is uncertain and uncomfortable.

A woman had a little poodle that died. A friend offered to give her another poodle. She replied, ''No, I never want another poodle. I don't want to go through any more sorrow.'' She did not realize that she was cutting herself off from joy and pleasure! If you are not willing to take the risk of being a friend, you will miss the joy of friendship.

To their credit, at least these three friends realized that Job needed them. Christ has a special place for friends who visit people. In talking about the last judgment, Jesus described a humble, self-effacing man who will be waiting for judgment. Jesus will say to him, ''I was sick and you visited me.''

The man will answer, ''I visited some people nobody cared about and nobody was interested in, but I do not remember visiting You, Lord.''

Then that man will be honored because he visited someone in need. He cared. He went.

Friends Without Equipment

Job's friends endure the agony of his suffering. They wait seven long days and nights in silence. They empathize with the pain he feels. Why do they fail him? They fail Job because they *do not have adequate resources*.

They are not equipped for the situation! Because they do not know what to say, their words are "full of sound and fury, signifying nothing." By saying the wrong things, they only compound Job's dilemma. Job says, "You, my friends, are like a stream. When the sun is blazing down on my swollen lips and parched throat, and I would give anything for some cool, clean water, I go to the stream and find it dry." He adds, "In the wintertime, when it is raining and the snow is melting, when the streams are crystal-clear, cool, and bountiful, I have no need of water. This is the way it has been with your friendship. We have had great times together. We have celebrated and feasted together. Our families have had fellowship and fun together. While the sun was shining, everything was beautiful. But now, when everything is dark and I am dying, you come as my friends but have nothing to give me."

Recently I was having trouble with my air-conditioning system. The repair center sent out two men in a big, efficient-looking truck. They used all kinds of equipment as they looked for the problem. When they finally found it, not only did they lack the right part to fix it, but they did not even know how to do the work. They informed me that the needed repair required someone else's expertise!

These men had shown up and examined everything, but they did not have the resources to tackle the problem. Although Job's friends listen and make beautiful speeches, they cannot minister to Job's needs because they do not have the right equipment.

Job says simply and plainly, "I know I am not a perfect man." Never does he say that he is without sin. Instead, he acknowledges the sin in his life and confesses it. He makes sacrifices for his sin and seeks the mind of God. He really does not know what he has done! He pleads, "Dear friends, please tell me what it is: however low, however horrible, however heinous it is. Just tell me what I have done."

Instead, the friends keep on goading Job to give up the facade of innocence and to confess. "Job, you certainly know what it is! Go ahead and tell us. Get it out of the way so you can die in peace."

Job responds, "I am tired of hearing you say that. Tell me something new, or just be quiet."

Friends Without a Watch

Not only do Job's friends not have adequate resources, but they also do not know when to leave. A friend of mine was in the hospital. Another friend had the idea that what the patient really needed was music. This well-meaning friend smuggled a quartet into the hospital to sing for our sick buddy. Later he told me that he thought the singers would never quit and go home! "Unfortunately," he said, "I survived."

We must have discernment when visiting people who are in need, or who are sick, or who have experienced the death of a loved one. Most of the time we talk too much and stay too long, as did Job's friends. They simply "wore out their welcome."

How do you minister to others when tragedy strikes? You may be asked to respond to a need in your own family, or outside it. Suffering comes to all, as does disaster and tragedy. Will you know what to say when someone tragically loses a loved one? What will you say to a dying friend? What will you do when someone close to you is without work and financial support? How will you respond?

A Friend Who Has It All

In crisis situations we should do all we can to provide assistance physically. But there is another dimension of help which we desperately need in our minds and hearts. These resources come from the Scriptures and from Jesus Christ, Who is our suffering Savior. We can share a word of hope and the assurance that Jesus experienced suffering, and that He understands. He has been there!

Some years ago Dr. Paul Brand visited a leper colony in Vellore, India. At that time no one wanted to minister to lepers, so they were isolated in seclusion in a large colony. Dr. Brand, a godly surgeon, went to work among them for a brief period.

When he arrived, the directors of the colony sat him down on a small mat in the middle of a circle. They gathered the patients to greet him, and then they all began to sing. Dr. Brand said he noticed that most of them were hiding their hands. Many had the clawlike hands which are typical of advanced leprosy. Some had only stubs of hands remaining; others had lost their fingers or their fingernails. Some sat on their hands or hid them behind their backs. Following the music, Dr. Brand was introduced as a famous Christian surgeon.

As Dr. Brand stood, translators prepared to deliver his remarks in two different dialects. Suddenly everything inside him went dry. He said, "I didn't have a message. I didn't know what to say to these forgotten, suffering nobodies." He prayed, "Lord, help me to say something which will bless them."

He began, "I am a hand surgeon. When I go into a group, the first thing I notice are the hands of people. I have spent my life studying the hand. I can look at your hands and tell what your vocation is by observing the location of calluses on your hands, the condition of your fingernails, and the softness or the toughness of your hands."

Dr. Brand continued, "Oh, how I would love to have seen the hands of Jesus Christ!" He talked about Jesus' hands as a baby, soft and helpless. Then he talked about the hands of Jesus as He was a boy going to school in the synagogue. He described how Jesus would pick up the stylus and write the alphabet. He continued, "I would like to have seen Jesus' hands when, as a carpenter, His fingernails were probably split and dirty, and there were scars from cuts and bruises He had gotten while working so hard during those years."

He told of the Master's hands when He was the Great Physician who healed the sick. His carpenter's hands must have grown softer every day as he shared His healing touch with people who needed Him. What hands He must have had when He rode into Jerusalem that Palm Sunday guiding an unbroken donkey colt!

"Then, from my experience as a hand surgeon," Dr. Brand continued, "I thought of the same hands with spikes driven into them. As a doctor, I know what happens when a spike is driven into a hand: It punctures tendons and muscles and blood vessels. You cannot drive a spike through a hand without deforming it. The hand would become clawlike. Jesus' hands were crippled and nailed to that cross as He identified with your suffering!"

As He looked at the hands of those lepers, he continued, "I would love to have seen His resurrected hands. Do you remember how He appeared in the upper room, clothed in His resurrected body? Do you think of a body with no flaws? Not so! One flaw remained. He said to Thomas, 'Put your fingers here; see My hands.' Evidently Jesus kept those scars so that in our suffering we will always know that Jesus identifies with us."

When Dr. Brand finished, he sat down on his little mat. Those who had been hiding their hands folded them in the Indian custom denoting applause. They honored Dr. Brand and they honored the Lord Jesus Christ as they said, "Thank You, Jesus, the Great Physician."

What can we say to someone in need, someone suffering, someone dying, someone confused? What can we say to those we love in their moment of crisis? We can say to them with love, "What a friend we have in Jesus!"

Chapter Insights

1. Job's well-meaning friends were of no help to him because they did not have adequate spiritual resources.
2. Job's dilemma was compounded by friends who did not know when to leave.
3. God alone supplies the consolation and empathy which is needed in an hour of darkness. "Though I dwell in darkness, the Lord is a light for me" (Micah 7:8 NASB).

5

Laughter in a Strange Place

He will yet fill your mouth with laughter and your lips with shouts of joy (Job 8:21).

I have become a laughingstock to my friends, though I called upon God and he answered—a mere laughingstock, though righteous and blameless! (Job 12:4).

When I smiled at them, they scarcely believed it; the light of my face was precious to them (Job 29:24).

• • • • •

After Eliphaz concludes that Job's suffering must be the result of his sin, Job gives a lengthy answer (chapters 6, 7). Then Bildad the Blaster commences his tirade. "You're nothing but a pious old windbag. You've spoken many words, but you don't know what they mean. You don't know what you're talking about!" Then he asks, "Is God good?" and answers with his own rhetoric:

"Yes, God is good. Can God do anything contrary to His character? No, God cannot do anything contrary to His character. Therefore, Job, when all your children were killed, God was behind it. Your children must have been very, very evil." Bildad is the friend who takes no prisoners; he tears Job limb from limb!

Then Zophar the Zealous takes his turn at bat, and guess who is the ball?

Admittedly, some of the logic of Job's friends makes sense. What then is wrong with the counsel they offered? It is not so much what they say as how they say it and what they leave out. Omission is the real problem. They forget that Job is a suffering man, living in turmoil and pain.

Perspective of Pain

My wife will testify that when I am sick, I am a bear. She puts a bell beside my bed, which I ring constantly! It sounds as loud as the Liberty Bell echoing through the house. I complain, "Where were you? What took you so long? My fever has gone up, and I'm hungry. No, I think I want juice. This room is hot! No, I want water." I have every complaint imaginable. The higher my fever goes and the sicker I become, the harder I am to live with. I get mad at everyone, including the germs. I say things that do not make any sense, because of my state of mind and body. My perspective becomes distorted.

Gratefully, my family usually makes allowances for my bad disposition when I don't feel well. Probably your family does the same for you. Our families compensate for us at such times by saying, "He didn't mean that" or "He had a bad day because he really doesn't feel well. He's not himself."

In contrast, Job's friends make no allowance for his feelings. They take his words literally and attack him at every turn. They forget a basic tenet: When a person experiences severe and brutal pain, he is not particularly interested in the world around him. His pain becomes an exclusive concern; manners, courtesy, and protocol are quickly set aside. Even God is sublimated when a person is preoccupied with pain.

The friends do not understand that Job's words come from a man who is in the grip of excruciating, deathlike pain. That is their first mistake!

Their second mistake results from their unbalanced theology. Eliphaz talks about the justice and righteousness of God, but he never mentions His mercy and grace. How we should thank God for the forgiveness, understanding, and patience of a loving heavenly Father! A lopsided theology is a precarious base for any argument, and Eliphaz's credibility suffers greatly because he is not practical in what he believes about God.

C. H. Spurgeon once noted the weakness of theologians who had this tendency. He said that he knew individuals who carried around theological revolvers in their ecclesiastical trousers, ready to assassinate someone over any petty detail! That was one of the problems with the logic of Job's friends. What they said, as far as they went, was fairly accurate. But even though it was based on accepted tradition, history, and revelation, it simply did not go far enough.

Another error in the teachings of these three friends was their lack of emphasis on prayer. The book of Job is a book of prayer. Prayers are found throughout its chapters, except in the comments of these three friends. They did not pray for or with Job. Never did they seek the counsel of God, for they already knew all the answers. Eliphaz, Bildad, and Zophar believed that they knew everything about God, about life, and about suffering. If they had all the answers, why should they talk to God? There is no hint or suggestion of prayer in their orations. They made a tragic mistake by trying to help Job without consulting God.

Satan Versus God

In the crisis of Job's life, as in most of life's crises, two purposes were involved. We are allowed to see this in Job's story only because the veil of history has been pushed back. We also need to see something of these dual purposes in our own lives when calamity strikes.

First, there was the purpose of Satan: to break Job physically with pain. The sarcasm and the ridicule of wife and friends were tools in Satan's hands, used to break Job's mental toughness and to crush him emotionally. Satan tried to use the silence of God to completely destroy Job's faith.

The Purpose of God

God wanted to teach Job some things about life

which he could never learn any other way. Someone who has come through a great trial knows about life and about God's faithfulness in a way that other people cannot understand.

Also, God wanted to use Job's life before all the principalities and powers of the universe as an illustration to refute Satan and his claims. In addition, all the generations which have followed have learned from the life of Job. Because of his example, when privation and hardship and trials come, men will experience the truth of Romans 8:38,39. We can be confident that nothing will happen to us which God does not allow and use for our good and for His glory. When suffering comes, we should understand both the destructive purposes of Satan and the enabling purposes of God.

What Makes You Laugh?

In the middle of Bildad's speech in chapter 8, we encounter an astounding thought in verse 21. Bildad tells Job, "He will yet fill your mouth with laughter and your lips with shouts of joy."

As you search the book of Job you will find that every page is wet with tears. Therefore it is surprising that *laughter* is mentioned more often in Job than in any other book in the Bible! The line between a tear and a smile, between joy and sorrow, is a thin one indeed. Laughter and sorrow are both necessary parts of life.

We should feel sorry for people who do not know how to laugh! We all know people who were born blind, and that is a great tragedy. Some people are unable to appreciate art, while others have no understanding of music. These may be difficult limitations, but none of them compare with the inability to laugh. To miss out on laughter is to miss out on one of the greatest gifts that God has given to His children.

Did you know that a human being is the only animal with the capacity to laugh? You might ask, "What about a hyena?" When a hyena does try to laugh, the end result is atrocious! We may have pets who can run and romp and hunt with us, but those pets are not able to laugh. Laughter is a real test of our character. Tell me what makes you laugh, and I will learn much about you.

Are you able to laugh at yourself? When you do something foolish or ridiculous, can you laugh about it? Those who can laugh at themselves, or those who can participate in a contest and see someone else win what they wanted to win, and can still laugh about it, are healthy folks. Being able to laugh at yourself says volumes about a solid self-image. On the contrary, if you can't laugh at yourself, you have problems with feelings of insecurity.

Not Worth a Dime!

Many different kinds of laughter appear in the story of Job. There is spontaneous, upbeat laughter; there is also the ridiculing, vicious kind. This cruel kind of laughter is mentioned in 12:4. Job accuses his friends, "You have made me the laughingstock!" Job is a respectable and wealthy man; he is also intelligent and godly. When people have problems, they come to him for consultation. When death comes in the community, Job has the healing word for the widow.

When his own calamity strikes, however, Job is labeled a hypocrite—"not worth a dime." Instead of the young men respectfully standing up when Job enters the room (as they once had), now they just laugh at him in merciless scorn.

A lad from a destitute family always arrived at school barefoot, in tattered, dirty clothes. The children would laugh at him, taunting, "Here comes dirty Charlie!" How cruel children can be! How cruel adults can be with some of their humor!

Laughter is a favorite weapon of Satan. If you go to a cocktail party and say, "No, thank you, I'll have a Coke," someone will sneer, "You don't drink? What's the matter? You mean you don't drink at all? Would you believe this guy?" The crowd roars with laughter at the person who lives his convictions.

Of one of his characters Dickens wrote, "She never laughs and seldom smiles, but when she smiles, it is sadder than most people's tears." Would you want to know such a woman? See the cruelty in that cynical statement. The meanest way Satan can attack a life is through ridicule!

Jonathan Swift's writings are an example of this kind of cynical, cruel humor. Thackeray, in *The English Humorist*, said that Swift was a giant literary figure in the English world. "When he died," said Thackeray, "It was like the falling of an empire." But he also observed that Swift's humor was sick. It was biting and sarcastic, and was written from a posture of superiority. That is a tragic kind of humor.''

God's Laughter

Laughter can also be used as an offensive weapon for God. Jesus used humor all the time. In Matthew 23:23,24 He accused the Pharisees of being blind men who majored on minors: ''You get upset about the little things that do not matter, but the big things do not bother you.'' He illustrated: ''You take your wine and carefully strain every tiny gnat out of it. You are so bothered by such a minute speck, but when a camel falls in your wine, you swallow hoof, legs, head, and humps.'' What a ridiculous picture! Jesus used humor to show those religious hypocrites that they were dealing with unimportant matters and missing the greatness of God.

Then there is the laughter of encouragement. Job said, ''I smiled at them when they did not believe, and the light of my face they did not cast down'' (29:24 NASB). In other words, when privation comes, the person who knows God can stand up in the middle of the storm and laugh because he is confident that God is in charge of the affairs of this world. After all, if God is for us, who can be against us? We spread good cheer with that confident smile.

Laughter in and of itself is neither good nor evil. It depends upon how and when it is used, and upon the person who uses it or the person who responds to it. A person who listens to and tells dirty stories, filled with vulgarity and immorality, has a mind filled with rubbish. The man whose thoughts concern that which is good and pure finds little humor in trash!

Will Rogers had an infectious, amiable kind of humor. He had the ability to tell jokes about well-known personalities, and they would feel flattered to be a part of his material. They knew that Will was telling his stories from a heart that loved America and genuinely cared about the people in his tales.

Once Will Rogers entertained some children in an orphanage with his famous rope tricks and funny stories. He had the youngsters rolling in the aisles with laughter! They were thrilled by the great entertainer. After intermission, the master of ceremonies could not find the star. He finally found Will Rogers in a corner, with his head in his hands, crying his heart out. "Mr. Rogers, what's the matter?" he inquired.

Will replied, "I'm sorry, but when I look at those pitiful children, it breaks my heart."

What a thin line between laughter and tears! You can laugh with someone who laughs at you, as long as you know that this person cares about you. But the cutting, biting laughter of rebuke and humiliation is disastrous.

A Little Bit of Honey

Genesis 43 tells of famine which has blighted the land of Canaan. Jacob assembles his sons to discuss how the family is to survive the food shortage. "You're going to have to go to Egypt and buy grain from that prime minister once more.'' Then they remind their father that Benjamin will have to go in order to prove that they were telling the truth. They do not know that the prime minister is their long-lost, supposedly dead brother whom they had thrown into a pit. After much persuading and convincing, Jacob agrees to let Benjamin go. He gives specific instructions as to what his sons would take with them. ''Take some fruit in the vessels, the best fruit in the land. Take myrrh. Take almonds. Take balm. Take pistachio nuts. And take some sweets with you. Take a little bit of honey.''

What good advice! We can spiritualize the text a little. In the humdrum of life you will get bored, and people will probably run over you. You may feel as though you're going to drown in the quicksand of the ''oughts'' and ''shoulds'' of life. In all the great and terrible things that happen, as well as in the petty mundane, I do not know of anything more needed than that ''little bit of honey.'' A smile or a laugh always helps.

You say, ''I have trouble laughing.'' Do you know why? Maybe it's because He who puts laughter in your heart and in your mouth is not ruling your life. The One who gives joy and zest to our lives is Jesus Christ, our Savior and Lord. One of the most precious gifts which He gives to us as His children is the ability to laugh at the right things at the right times.

Do you know the Lord, Jesus Christ? Is He really in your heart and life? If so, He will fill your mouth with laughter and your life with His special brand of joy!

Chapter Insights

1. Job's friends were not helpful because they could not see from his perspective.
2. The source of laughter can always be discerned by its effect and purpose.
   a. If it is used to ridicule and belittle, it is Satan's destructive tool.
   b. If it is used to encourage and enjoy, it is God's offensive weapon.

6
The Underdog

Doubtless you are the people, and wisdom will die with you! But I have a mind as well as you; I am not inferior to you. Who does not know all these things? I have become a laughingstock to my friends, though I called upon God and he answered—a mere laughingstock, though righteous and blameless! Men at ease have contempt for misfortune as the fate of those whose feet are slipping (Job 12:2-5).

• • • • •

Is it true that when a man falters, there are blows for him? When someone is down, will he be kicked? Job is an underdog, and he believes this idea. He tells us that everyone is kicking him because of his misfortune. Is it so unusual for the wounded to be kicked? No. It happens every day!

Suppose two men are talking to you at the same time. One man is telling you how he struck out while the other is telling you how he hit a home run. One man is telling you how he fumbled and the other how he scored a touchdown. Which man has your interest?

We love and even worship success in our culture. On the contrary, when someone is down and out, we tend to kick him with either contempt or apathy.

When I was a boy, I remember seeing a classic Western. It was classic because both Randolph Scott and John Wayne starred in the same movie. In the plot, both of them were "good guys," but they had very different personalities. Both were after the same girl and the same cattle ranch. Their goals were identical.

At the end of the movie, Randolph Scott and John Wayne were in a big fight scene. They were going at it tooth-and-nail. What a fight! The broken props and smashed windows in that one scene must have cost those Hollywood producers a fortune. Men were thrown over the bar and hit over the head. One man and then the other would go down. They crashed through the barroom door and staggered into the muddy street and kept fighting. As I recall, John Wayne lost that fight. He was outclassed!

Then the crowd picked up the winner and carried him off on their shoulders. They left John Wayne lying unconscious where he had fallen. Obviously, he was the one who needed to be carried. But with shouts of victory they chose the man who won the fight. That is just the way our world works! We honor the hero or the heroine and we send the loser stumbling into oblivion. Underdogs do get kicked.

Some time ago our family went to the beach for our vacation. One afternoon Ben and Cliff came to our room and said, "Dad, you will never guess who we met on the beach! We've been with him for two or three hours...Sylvester Stallone!"

"As in *Rocky*?"

"Yes! We were right there with him. His wife was there too, and they were swimming! And we talked to his bodyguard."

For four days my boys went to the beach to see Rocky. They had a new story every day.

"You should see him! He must work out all the time! He has the best tan on the beach!"

"How do people respond to him?" I asked one day.

"Oh, they walk by and ask for his autograph, and they want to take his picture. He tries to be nice, but they won't leave him alone."

Then I asked Ben and Cliff how *they* acted.

"We've worked our way into his group and we sunbathe at the same place with him. And we talk some."

I had to check this out for myself. As I sat on the beach, along came Rocky. He was handsome all right, but Sylvester Stallone had a humble, quiet way about him. He handled himself on a public beach with real class.

All eyes on the beach were staring at Rocky! Whether he was swimming or sunbathing, people could not keep their eyes or conversation off the celebrity. They flocked around him. It was amazing.

Up the beach was another man who evidently

had suffered either a stroke or some kind of paralysis. I watched him as he laboriously made his way into the water, step-by-step. It was easy to forget all about the movie star and his entourage as I watched that broken man concentrate with great effort on every movement of his body.

I wanted to get to know that man, and so I talked with him and heard his story. He was lonely and hungry for a friend. This man needed a word of encouragement and recognition. He needed to know that he counted for something. If Rocky just said hello to anyone in the crowd, that person would be willing to spend the day at his side. But the afflicted man was ignored completely.

If that man had spoken to anyone on the beach, he probably would have been shunned. People would have politely withdrawn from him, passing by on the other side. No one would have wanted to hurt him, but by neglect the underdog would have been kicked again. But in my opinion the real star of the beach was the paralyzed man! He went into the water with great determination and courage.

Vulnerability Invites Abuse

Job discovers that when a person is hurting, he is more likely to be abused. If someone other than Job had said this, we might dismiss it with a suggestion that the person is just covering up his weaknesses.

We commonly attack other people in areas where we feel deficient ourselves. Jesus told about the man who had a two-by-four in his eye and made an issue of a tiny speck in someone else's eye. Jesus said that the two-by-four was causing great blindness in the eye of the critic, so that he could not see his own deficiency.

This is not true of Job. He is not a whiner. He is a ministering and loving person who cares for other people. Because he is the one who is suffering, he looks like a loser as people kick him. Some do it with verbal contempt, others with neglect and ridicule, and still others with destructive criticism and advice. Job understands how it feels to be kicked. He says, "I have suffered my way to that conclusion. I have been there, and in fact I am there right now."

Exceptions to the Rule

Fortunately, not everyone kicks the underdog! There are many in Christ's family who have given years of their lives to ministering to suffering humanity. They give of their time and money. They reach out to help someone who is having a difficult time financially, or to someone in poor health, or to someone whose family life is in crisis. This response, however, is the exception and not the rule. What causes such people to be so different from the run-of-the-mill person? What is their secret?

Most people would conclude that losers do not amount to much and simply need to be counted out or be passed over. Adolph Hitler was not the first world leader who executed people because of their weaknesses. Weakness is often considered the unpardonable sin, even on primary school playgrounds.

A prominent scholar was in dialogue with a group of student theologians. The brilliant man had written many books. Most of the students were intelligent and well-read. One of the students was not as bright or sharp as the others. His clothes, his manners, and his speech clearly revealed his limitations. In spite of this, his fellow students knew him to be a fine, genuine Christian. He loved his Lord with a simple, basic faith that could not be ignored.

In the middle of the dialogue, this student asked a simple question. He sincerely wanted to know the answer to a very basic question. But instead of being civil to him, the great scholar was vicious. He did not stop until he had totally humiliated the young man.

The room became so quiet you could hear a pin drop! The students immediately changed their opinion of that prominent scholar. They were embarrassed for their friend and protective of him. While on his way to making a point, the erudite scholar lost the respect of the group because he had kicked the underdog in the presence of his friends.

Reasons and Excuses

Why do people kick underdogs? One of the reasons is that we worship success and despise failure. If someone tries to tell us how he lost money on an investment, we are not interested. However, if someone wants to tell us how he got rich overnight on an investment, we would pay a hundred dollars to listen to him!

Job was a man of prestige in his earlier years. Now he knows the other side of the coin. In his suffering he feels loneliness, neglect, and ridicule. Job discovers to his dismay that when someone falls down, he *will* be kicked.

Since we mortals do worship success, we also kick underdogs because we believe that stepping on an underdog will elevate us and make us "top dogs"! We continually try to build up ourselves by tearing down someone else.

In Luke 18:10-13 Jesus related the parable about the Pharisee who went into the temple to worship. He said, "Lord, how fortunate You are to have a man like I am who is moral, so ethical, so handsome, so intelligent, so godly, so perfect. Oh, how wonderful I am!" It helped that Pharisee's egotistical prayer to be able to point to a poor, immoral publican in the temple. "God, please take note: I am better than other men."

In James 2:1-9 the author warns about our identification with "movers and shakers." He says, "When someone of wealth comes to church, we say, 'Come in, sir. We have saved a seat for you right here at the front. Would you move over, little lady? Son, step aside. Come right here, sir. Certainly we have room for you.' " James goes on to say that when the underdog arrives, we direct him to a balcony seat in the back. "You can see fairly well if you have good eyesight!"

We worship prominence and position. When someone wins an election, it does not matter how unscrupulous the means to the end might have been—a politician will still be applauded because he has achieved a position of power. All want to join his team. Job learned something about the treatment of underdogs when he found himself at the bottom of the ladder. Before he was in the gutter, Job had not known how it felt to be down and out. Afterward, he knew!

Avoiding Reality

There is still another reason for kicking underdogs: We do not want to face unpleasant and distasteful situations if we can possibly avoid them. Consider the way some people deal with drug addicts or alcoholics. They step back and say, "Nobody made this man drink or become dependent on drugs. I am surely not going to get involved with him." When we do not want to get our hands dirty, or our hearts involved by loving and helping, we back away.

If someone in the church is trapped in an immoral situation, the last people who want to be identified with this individual are his brothers and sisters in Christ. We bury our self-righteous heads in the sand and abandon such persons. Someone wisely observed that the Christian army is the only army in the world that shoots its wounded. Too many times this is true.

In the midst of all his suffering, Job grapples with this principle. He says, "I am down. I am finished. I am through. I want to die. Nobody loves me or cares enough to help."

Becoming an underdog only compounds Job's suffering. Additional pain is heaped upon a person who is already hurting! New waves of heartache swell up. Why does suffering compound itself with these new and unnecessary sources of pain?

Years ago a very brilliant young man was called to pastor in a tough situation. He was sent to minister to slaves who were living as captives on the outskirts of Babylon. Those men and women had lost their faith in God because their religion had been tied to the land they had to give up. Forced to leave their homeland, the captives had been taken to a strange land, where they were forced to live as slaves and servants. Their sense of family and heritage had been lost. They were impoverished spiritually, emotionally, and physically.

Before this new pastor named Ezekiel could minister to his people, he had to "sit where they sat." He had to empathize and to know about their perspective. Ezekiel knew that he did not have the right to open his mouth until he had identified totally with their suffering. He cried their tears and he felt their pain. Only then could he help to lift their burden. He identified with their plight. He said, "I sat where they sat."

Ministry to Underdogs

We touch the lives of underdogs all the time. They are the unsuccessful ones, the ones who have not quite made it, the ones who have reached for the stars and have ended up with a handful of mud. We go to school with them, work with them, and see them at church every week. They have failed and have been passed over because of unsolved problems. What do we do when we touch the lives of such people? Are we sensitive? Can we say with Ezekiel, "I sat where they sat"? There is only one way to learn how to love and to touch underdogs: by suffering yourself!

A Christian professor of sociology once said, "It takes five resounding, painful failures to produce greatness in a man's life." To have compassion for an underdog, a person must experience suffering. Because Job knew suffering firsthand, he would never treat an underdog in the same way!

People respond to suffering in different ways. Some develop a martyr complex. These poor souls are in ecstasy when they can share their agony: "Let me tell you about *my* surgery and the terrible ordeal I have been through! There has never been an operation like mine in the history of the world!"

For others, suffering makes them hard and unsympathetic because they are diligently trying to prove their own self-sufficiency. They say, "You have to stand up under it." In contempt they say to the underdog, "You just fight your way through." They show no sensitivity to those who are hurting. These same folks are good at mistaking self-will for courage.

In contrast, suffering can make human beings far more gentle and tender. They have a new sympathy born out of their own experiences. That result is what God wants from every one of us. In the face of suffering, it is His expressed and perfect will that we develop the mind and the heart of the Great Physician, Jesus Christ.

Consider this passage from Philippians 2:4-8: "Do not merely look out for your own personal interests, but also for the interests of others" (NASB). Paul is saying, "Be sensitive to those in need." He then explains how we develop this sensitivity: "Have this attitude in yourselves which was also in Christ Jesus, who, although He existed in the form of God, did not regard equality with God a thing to be grasped, but emptied Himself, taking the form of a bond-servant, and being made in the likeness of men. And being found in appearance as a man, He humbled Himself by becoming obedient to the point of death, even death on a cross" (NASB).

It is important to recognize that the very Son of God *deliberately* endured the deepest levels of suffering to *deliberately* become the underdog of the world! He suffered the pain of the nails and of the crown of thorns when His skin was ripped to shreds. That was not enough. He knew what it was to be spit upon. His ears were filled with the curses of those who had no sympathy for His physical pain. He knew ridicule, and the abject pain of loneliness and rejection when He felt forsaken by His Father. No man could identify with Him as He hung on the cross alone.

Our Lord knew all of this for a very special reason that the writer of Hebrews explains in 2:18: "For since He Himself was tempted in that which He has suffered, He is able to come to the aid of those who are tempted" (NASB). Christ suffered the pain of the underdog so He might come to our aid! If such a price was required of the Son of God, consider the value of suffering for us.

How do you keep from kicking the underdog? You identify with him. You sit where he sits for a while. You suffer for a while yourself, and then you are able to really love, to really minister. You become like your Master. Thank God for the sensitive members of His family! Like Ezekiel, those Christians *feel* the pain before they speak of it. Often they can empathize because they have gone through their own pain, and because of it they have a special ministry. They come to the aid of people when others ignore them. How precious they are to God!

Chapter Insights

1. A person usually puts down another human being in an effort to elevate or inflate his own sagging ego.
2. Suffering is often a prerequisite for genuine compassion because it allows one person to identify with the pain of another.
3. Suffering either hardens or softens the human heart. Experience suffering and you will be changed!

7

One Minute After Death

If only you would hide me in the grave and conceal me till your anger has passed! If only you would set me a time and then remember me! If a man dies, will he live again? All the days of my hard service I will wait for my renewal to come (Job 14:13,14).

I know that my Redeemer lives, and that in the end he will stand upon the earth. And after my skin has been destroyed, yet in my flesh I will see God; I myself will see him with my own eyes—I, and not another. How my heart yearns within me! (Job 19:25-27).

● ● ● ● ●

Imagine that you are lying in a hospital bed, kept alive by tubes connected to your nose and arm. As a result of a natural calamity, all of your family has been killed, and you are waiting to die. Everything you have ever worked for—savings, home, car—all is gone. No one comes to visit you in your loneliness, but you have reached the point in your suffering that you do not even care. You have totally given up on life, and have almost given up on God.

This is much like the graphic description of Job in chapters 12, 13, and 14. He defends himself against the charges of his three friends, and in his defense he accuses God. Job is neither patient nor impatient; he becomes violent toward the Almighty. Over and over again he shakes his fist at God and asks, "Why?" In response, the heavens are silent. He tries to bring God into a courtroom, but God will not be manipulated.

Then, in the midst of all the darkness and pessimism, we see in chapter 12 a little glimmer of light that is the reflection of a truth from chapter 9: Job appeals to God for a mediator. He feels a need for someone to stand between him and God to judge and interpret what is right and fair. Job concludes that if God cannot be understood, life is not worth living. Job cries out for an intercessor to make judgments and to give evidence of God's justice in the world.

These are strong words about God, but in spite of Job's harshness, there is a glimmer of a truth that will be developed in the New Testament. The need expressed by Job is the essence of what is needed between all sinful men and the one holy God. We see here the longing for Messiah, who can be God's Mediator with men. This is the beginning of a prophetic statement, found in the oldest book in all the Bible.

The Ultimate Question

Throughout the book of Job, deeply profound questions are asked: "Why did God create man in the first place? Can a man really know God? Does an infinite God care about finite man?"

In chapter 14 one of the most profound questions of all is posed: "If a man dies, will he live again?" Every person who has ever breathed has asked this same question! "After death, what happens to us?"

Even the atheist poet Edgar Allen Poe tried to answer Job's question. In his works Poe mirrored his life of drug addiction and alcoholism, a life that ended at the age of 40 in the gutter district of Baltimore. In one of his stories, Poe depicted a man strapped over a pit above which swung a gigantic pendulum with a razor-sharp blade. With every tick of the clock, the pendulum inched closer and closer to the suspended man. Similarly, Poe said, "I am strapped above the pit of eternity, and with every beat of my heart I am just that much closer to annihilation." If Poe had been asked the question, "If a man dies, will he live again?" he would have answered with a resounding "No!"

From another perspective, the humanist would have an answer different from that of the atheist. So many Easter sermons fit this mold. The philosopher/clergyman talks about the metamorphosis of caterpillar to butterfly and the divine spark in us all. He reassures his audience that merely hoping there is life hereafter will indeed make it so.

Still another view is the Hebrew understanding

of life after death. It is this perspective from which Job asks, "If a man dies, will he live again?" The Hebrews understood Sheol to be some sort of shadowy, purgatory-type existence that followed death and preceded the Messiah, who would come and ultimately be resurrected from the dead.

Job expresses his personal belief in this resurrection in 19:25-27:

> And as for me, I know that my Redeemer
> lives,
> And at the last He will take His stand on the
> earth.
> Even after my skin is destroyed,
> Yet from my flesh I shall see God,
> Whom I myself shall behold,
> And whom my eyes shall see and not another
> (NASB).

If Job clearly understands and believes that there will be a resurrection, why does he ask the question?

Look at it again: "If a man dies, will he live again?" The word "again" was added by the translators to make the passage more understandable, but in fact it has complicated Job's question. He is not asking, "If I die, or if you die, will we live at another time?" He is simply asking, "After a man dies, does he sleep in his body for a long time, or float around in some kind of shadowy existence or limbo?"

Many of us are as ignorant as Job about the details of life after death. This question must be answered in the light of New Testament teaching. What did Jesus say about this? What did Paul teach? If a man dies, *is he still living*? At the very moment he leaves his earthly existence, *what happens to him*?

The question is about the continuity of life. To probe into the realm of the supernatural is to get into deep water. What about babies who have died? What about children in the resurrection? What about life after death for those who were buried at sea? How important are our bodies to the afterlife? What about those who were in horrible automobile accidents, or those who were in explosions, whose bodies disintegrated?

To face the complexity of the question, consider the case of Roger Williams. Williams, an early Baptist preacher and the founder of Rhode Island, was buried with great reverence by his peers. Years later they exhumed his body in order to move it. When they uncovered his casket, they discovered that the roots from an apple tree had grown through the casket and into the skull. The root of the apple tree had wound itself around his spine, down into his hip area. Then separate roots had grown around his right and left leg bones.

The chemicals from the body of Roger Williams had passed into the root of that apple tree. They were carried up into the trunk, the limbs, the branches, and into the apples themselves. When people ate apples from that tree, though they did not know it, they were eating elements from Roger Williams' body! Job's question was indeed filled with complexities!

What is the Christian answer? It is found in 1 Corinthians 15:35-49. Paul expands Job's question. He begins by asking two additional questions, and then he gives three analogies and four contrasts.

But someone will say, "How are the dead raised? And with what kind of body do they come?" You fool! That which you sow does not come to life unless it dies; and that which you sow, you do not sow the body which is to be, but a bare grain, perhaps of wheat or of something else. But God gives it a body just as He wished, and to each of the seeds a body of its own.

All flesh is not the same flesh, but there is one flesh of men, and another flesh of beasts, and another flesh of birds, and another of fish. There are also heavenly bodies and earthly bodies, but the glory of the heavenly is one, and the glory of the earthly is another. There is one glory of the sun, and another glory of the moon, and another glory of the stars; for star differs from star in glory.

So also is the resurrection of the dead. It is sown a perishable body, it is raised an imperishable body; it is sown in dishonor, it is raised in glory; it is sown in weakness, it is raised in power; it is sown a natural body, it is raised a spiritual body. If there is a natural body, there is also a spiritual body.

So also it is written, "The first man, Adam, became a living soul." The last Adam became a life-giving spirit. However, the spiritual is not first, but the natural; then the spiritual. The first man is from the earth, earthy; the second man is from heaven.

As is the earthy, such also are those who are earthy; and as is the heavenly, so also are those who are heavenly. And just as we have borne the image of the earthy, we shall also bear the image of the heavenly (NASB).

Paul presents the analogies of a seed, of flesh, and of planets. His four contrasts begin with the perishable compared to the imperishable. Second, he contrasts that which is dishonored with that which is glorified. Next, he contrasts that which is weak with that which is powerful. Finally, he contrasts that which is natural with that which is spiritual.

These analogies and contrasts must be understood so that we can grasp his answer. Beginning in 1 Corinthians 15:35, Paul answers two questions he had been asked by cynics in Corinth. The first question: "How are the dead raised?" The second: "What kind of body do they have when they come forth from the dead?"

He answers the first question in verse 36. It was a philosophical question. We can almost feel the cynicism, the sarcasm, of the Greeks who asked it, seeking to stump Paul: "Tell us, Paul, just how are the dead raised?"

The Greeks were extremely verbose and were throwing out words in a cynical way: "How can someone who is dead come back to life again? That is ridiculous!"

Paul replies, "You fools! That which you sow does not come to life unless it dies. What a foolish question. Go ask the dumbest farmer in Corinth, and he can answer that! Nothing is resurrected unless there is death. A seed is placed in the soil and covered with dirt. Then the rains come and the sun shines. The seed has to die before there can be a resurrection as a plant. This is common knowledge. The whole thrust of nature teaches that death begins the process of resurrection."

Their second question is, "What kind of body will they have?" If a man dies, shall he live? Oh, yes! But *how* shall he live? What kind of existence will he have? Is it some shadowy thing? Some form of purgatory? Does the soul simply sleep?

"No," says Paul. It is at this point that he presents the three analogies and the four contrasts. The first analogy, in verses 37 and 38, refers to seed grain: "When you sow, you do not plant the body that will be, but just a seed, perhaps of wheat or of something else. But God gives it a body as he has determined, and to each kind of seed he gives its own body."

The grain speaks of *continuity*. Inspired by the Holy Spirit, Paul is saying that our body is like a seed. When it dies, it is planted like a seed. That seed produces a plant, a tree, the resurrected body, the glorified body, the heavenly body. That body is related to the seed. There is continuity! If you plant wheat, wheat comes up. The wheat takes a different form from the seed, but there is continuity.

Consider his next analogy, given in verse 39: "All flesh is not the same: Men have one kind of flesh, animals have another, birds another, and fish another." This analogy of flesh talks about identity. The meat of a fowl is different from the meat of a fish. The flesh of an animal is different from the flesh of a man. All are different. Therefore, there will be *identity*.

There is continuity—the seed and the resurrected life. There is identity: The flesh we now have is connected to our resurrected bodies. We will know people. We will recognize people. The characteristics of our present lives will be carried over into our glorified bodies when we die.

The next analogy is in verses 40 and 41: "There are also heavenly bodies and there are earthly bodies; but the splendor of the heavenly bodies is one kind, and the splendor of the earthly bodies is another. The sun has one kind of splendor, the moon another, and the stars another; and star differs from star in splendor."

In this analogy of the planets, Paul points out that there will be *diversity*. In our glorified bodies there will be not only *continuity* and *identity*, but also *diversity*. We will not all sit in heaven and play harps. There will be progress, growth, creativity, diversity. Through these analogies, Paul describes important facts about our glorified bodies.

A Picture of Death

He then presented the contrasts, beginning in verse 42: "So will it be with the resurrection of the dead. The body that is sown is perishable, but it is raised imperishable."

In truth, we are all dying. We are closer to death today than we were yesterday. When we were born, we were infected with a terminal disease called "death." We are not as quick today as we were yesterday. We are not as sharp today as we were yesterday. There is a gradual (with some, a dramatic) deterioration of life. This old body is perishing! You can prop it up, you can put on glasses, you can change hairstyles, you can have your face lifted, but your body is dying. It is a perishable body.

Paul says we will have a body that is imperishable. What will that body be like? First John 3:2 says we will be like Jesus—*exactly* like Him! What was Jesus like in His glorified body? His body could appear and disappear. It would walk through walls. It had all the sensibility we now have, but it was heightened to an unbelievable extent. Adam, prior to his fall, had tremendous ability. Our glorified body will be something like the body that Adam would have now had he not sinned in the Garden. This is the analogy found in the latter part of this same chapter, when Paul wrote about the first Adam and the Second Adam, which is Jesus. The first Adam is earthly; the Second Adam is heavenly. We will take this old earthly Adam's body, and we will see it transformed into a new Adam's glorified body, fit for the heavenlies. What is sown is perishable; what is raised is imperishable.

In the next contrast (verse 43), the body is sown in dishonor but is raised in glory. There are a lot of scars on our bodies. Sin has scarred us deeply. Prior to the flood, the average life span was nearly a thousand years. If someone reaches the age of one hundred today, we are amazed. This is what sin has done to mortals.

A life span of a thousand years is nothing in God's timing! This old body is sown in dishonor. However, it will be *raised* a glorified body. That is the contrast presented in this verse.

In the latter part of verse 43, the next contrast is presented: "It is sown in weakness but raised in power." How weak this body is! Consider the weakness of a human body compared to that of animals. We are not strong at all. If someone weighs 110 pounds and can lift 200 pounds, we are impressed. But if we compare the body weight of a human to that of an ant, and then compare the weight each can lift, we are humbled. If an ant weighed what a human weighs, he would pick up half a ton with his teeth alone!

If grasshoppers were the size of humans, they would be able to leap 30 and 40 feet every time they took a step. We cannot hear as well as a dog. We do not have the sense of direction of a cat or a bird. How limited, how weak is this human body! Paul tells us that our new body will be raised in power!

Notice the final contrast in verse 44: "It is sown a natural body but raised a spiritual body." This old earthbound, limited body is to be raised a supernatural body.

We begin to see the total painting that Paul is placing on the canvas. He is portraying us as seeds sown and as plants produced. We have a continuity between this life and the next life, between this body and our glorified body. We have identity. We recognize one another.

The plants are another analogy. The light of the moon is different from the light of the sun. The light of the sun is different from that of the constellation Orion. There is *diversity*.

The contrasts are clear: When we sow what is perishable, a body which is imperishable comes up in the resurrection. When we sow this old body that has been dishonored, a body that has glory about it comes up. When we sow this old body in weakness, a body that is powerful replaces it. When we sow this natural, earthly body, a supernatural, spiritual body appears! It is going to be wonderful! We Christians will leave this limited life and go on to be with God in glory forever. We will know as we have been known. This is our faith! This is the confidence we have!

Yes, We Shall Live!

How shall we answer Job's question, "If a man dies, will he live?" We shall answer it with a resounding *Yes*!—if that man died in Christ. If he died *outside* Christ, will he live? The answer is still yes, but, as did Judas, he will go to "his own place." We go to our *own* place, according to our rejection of Jesus Christ, exactly as man has through the ages. If a man dies, will he live? Yes, he will live. He will either live with his glorified body in heaven or else he will live separated from God in hell.

Jesus answers this same question so simply. In John 11:25,26 He says, "I am the resurrection and the life. He who believes in me will live, even though he dies; and whoever lives and believes in me will never die. Do you believe this?"

The question we are grappling with is not just the question of Job, with his limited Old Testament understanding. The question before us is the question Jesus asked in John 11, *"Do you believe this?"* Do you believe it, or don't you? The difference between belief and unbelief is the difference between heaven and hell!

Chapter Insights

1. The question of life after death is not a matter of *whether*, but *where*.
2. We have the option to identify either with the first Adam, our earthly progenitor, or the Second Adam, our heavenly Lord and Savior.

8

The Silence of God

But if I go to the east, he is not there; if I go to the west, I do not find him. When he is at work in the north, I do not see him; when he turns to the south, I catch no glimpse of him (Job 23:8,9).

Men move boundary stones; they pasture flocks they have stolen. They drive away the orphan's donkey and take the widow's ox in pledge. They thrust the needy from the path and force all the poor of the land into hiding. Like wild donkeys in the desert, the poor go about their labor of foraging food; the wasteland provides food for their children. They gather fodder in the fields and glean in the vineyards of the wicked. Lacking clothes, they spend the night naked; they have nothing to cover themselves in the cold. They are drenched by mountain rains and hug the rocks for lack of shelter. The fatherless child is snatched from the breast; the infant of the poor is seized for a debt. Lacking clothes, they go about naked; they carry the sheaves, but still go hungry. They crush olives among the terraces; they tread the winepresses, yet suffer thirst. The groans of the dying rise from the city, and the souls of the wounded cry out for help. But God charges no one with wrongdoing (Job 24:2-13).

●　●　●　●　●

Job asks two more pivotal questions in chapters 23 and 24. First he asks, "Why is God absent from human affairs?" His second question is, "Why is God silent?" Job is lamenting, "If only I could bring my complaints before the Lord and state my case! If only He would listen to my plight and intervene on my behalf!"

In his distress over the apparent absence of God, Job feels abandoned and complains, "If I go to the east, he is not there; if I go to the west, I do not find him. When he is at work in the north, I do not see him; when he turns to the south, I catch no glimpse of him" (23:8,9). Always before, God had been available to Job. His was a familiar cry: "Where is God now, when I need Him?"

Job begins to build a case against God. First he points out the corruption in his society: "Men move boundary stones; they pasture flocks they have stolen. They drive away the orphan's donkey and take the widow's ox in pledge. They thrust the needy from the path" (24:2-4). He is saying, "God, these are despicable people who are ruling the world. Where are You while all this is taking place?"

Have you ever said that? Have you ever asked God why a drug pusher rides around in the lap of luxury while you struggle to survive? Is there no reward for being a conscientious, Bible-believing Christian?

Second, Job reflects on the plight of the poor: "[They] force all the poor of the land into hiding. Like wild donkeys in the desert, the poor go about their labor of foraging food; the wasteland provides food for their children. They gather fodder in the fields and glean in the vineyards of the wicked. Lacking clothes, they spend the night naked; they have nothing to cover themselves in the cold. They are drenched by mountain rains and hug the rocks for lack of shelter. The fatherless child is snatched from the breast...but God charges no one with wrongdoing" (24:4-9,12).

The absence and the silence of God baffle and astound Job, as well as those of us who live in this century.

Job's words, "Oh, if only I knew where to find Him!" emerge as both a sob and a prayer from his suffering lips. To locate and to know God has been the desire of men and women since the dawn of civilization. Haven't you prayed the very same prayer? We have reached out in the darkness of fear and despair and wept, "God, I am claiming all my reason for needing You! I am putting all my righteousness and prayers on the line. I am depending only on You. If ever I needed You, it is now. Come! Help! Assist! Touch! Heal! Give guidance! Please answer me!"

The philosopher goes about looking for God while the theologian stands on the authority of the Bible and declares that God is looking for man. There are times when we pray, "God, if You're

looking for me, here I am! I am not hiding any-
where. Please come find me!''

Paul's letter to the Romans pointedly says that
God is seeking to touch and to change all men and
women at all times, in all places, all over the world.
In fact, that is the thrust of the entire New Testament!

Why then, in Romans chapter 1, do we read
three times the sobering phrase ''God gave them
up''? How can a book be about God's persistent
love and yet begin with the statement ''God gave
them up''?

Every time we seek to build a case affirming that
God always listens, we discover that there is
another situation in which it seems that God is
silent. There is not even a whisper from Him! Just
as we are prepared to say, ''God is good and
righteous and just,'' we face a tragic situation that
forces us to question how God allows such things
to happen!

What is the answer? We face the same realities
of life as Job did. It is important for us to face
the silence of God at a time when we are reason-
ably sane and healthy, when we are able to think
and to pray about these perplexing circumstances.

Bewildering Reality

In the Garden of Eden, God told Adam and Eve
to ''Be fruitful and multiply, and fill the earth,
and subdue it'' (Genesis 1:28 NASB). Since that
day men have worked to find the tiny thread which
holds this universe together. Sir Isaac Newton
worked daily for over 20 years to reconcile one

tiny inconsistency in the basic laws of physics. How long did men freeze to death while sitting on enough coal to keep them warm for thousands of years? Their problem was not their need to discover coal; it was the need to discover the truth of what coal could do for them.

How much money has been spent trying to find an answer for cancer? What is it? What causes it? How is it cured?

Why hasn't God revealed all these mysteries to us? Why doesn't He just give us all the answers? Why is He silent and absent while we cry and agonize and feel alone in our pain? These were Job's questions, too!

A little girl was asked by her Sunday school teacher, "Mary, who made you?"

"God made part of me," she answered.

"Explain that for me," the teacher continued.

"Well, God made me little. And the rest of me—I just growed up myself!"

God gave us a beginning, but we must do something for ourselves! For example, God gave us the ability to dream. What would it be like if we had nothing to dream about? God has given us a passion for discovery. What if everything were already discovered? What would we do with our minds, with our ability to learn and grow? What if we had all truth already? Life would become a stagnant, boring, pointless grind. Perhaps the greatest truth we can discover is that there is something far more important than just living: It is the quality of the life we live that really counts. And this quality lies in "growing ourselves up" as we search for the secrets of the universe.

Someone said, "If I could catch all knowledge and truth and hold them in my hand, I would release it all so I might have the thrill of pursuing and trying to catch it again."

A world where all the answers have been found and all the solutions discovered would be dull indeed. It would be void of progress, growth, and life.

God wants us to know truth. Sometimes our complaints that God is hiding or that He is silent reveal the fact that we fear His answers!

Job was concerned about the truth that is related to pain—the same subject which Paul addressed centuries later. Paul sought similar answers as he begged God three times to remove his "thorn in the flesh."

> To keep me from exalting myself, there was given me a thorn in the flesh, a messenger of Satan to buffet me—to keep me from exalting myself! Concerning this I entreated the Lord three times that it might depart from me. And He has said to me, "My grace is sufficient for you, for power is perfected in weakness" (2 Corinthians 12:7-9 NASB).

Paul wanted to travel and write and preach and plant churches. And a sick person surely couldn't be of much use to God! But the Lord said no. Finally Paul figured out the truth about the thorn: His pain kept him on his knees; it kept him right with God; it made him grow spiritually. Pain made Paul a theologian, a writer, and the greatest missionary the world has ever known. It made him a real man of God!

Lessons from Dark Places

Nan Eidsen, a young girl around the turn of the century, was stricken with tuberculosis. The doctors feared for her life, so she was sent to a sanitarium for several years. During that time she visited and befriended almost every patient who came to that bleak place. Most of these were terminally ill patients, whom she watched die. Because of her own pain and suffering and through her daily exposure to others who were hurting and dying, she steadily grew stronger in the Lord.

In God's providence, Nan's condition began to improve. In that sanitarium she carved out a special place of ministry among dying patients. She came to them with the Bible and with love. Although she was just a young country girl, the love of Christ transcended Nan's pain. That same love drove her to share God's supernatural grace with those who hurt as she did. Pain was the common denominator, and it gave Nan a credibility she would not have had otherwise.

After she was cured, Nan studied nursing and eventually became director of the nursing school at the Baptist Hospital in Columbia, South Carolina. During the 40 years that Nan Eidsen held that position, she continued to go up and down the hospital corridors sharing the same kind of love and hope she had talked about in that sanitarium.

She is now in her eighties, working with swollen feet, arthritis, and all kinds of physical ailments. When there is an automobile accident or tragedy,

the emergency team will say, "Go get Miss Nan."
When a patient is dying and the family cannot
handle the inevitable, or when the doctor comes
out of surgery and tells the family there is nothing
that can be done, the physician or the nurse will
send for "Miss Nan."

Nan Eidsen can deal with pain and death because the territory is familiar. She is there with a
touch of Christ in a powerful ministry! The lifestyle of this dear saint is characterized by simplicity
and sacrifice. She has saved nothing of what she
has earned. All of her clothes are gifts from
churches. During the years that she taught Sunday
school, she gave her dresses to needy students in
her class, until she had nothing left to wear.
Finally, friends who gave Miss Nan the clothes
began to monogram her initials on them; but she
put patches over the initials and continued to give
them away!

Some Christians bought a little house for
her, and she even gave that away to a newly
married couple who worked at the hospital. She
preferred to stay in the old room at the hospital.

How did Miss Nan develop such a spirit? Much
of it came through the time when she was dying
with tuberculosis. God touched her when she was
hurting and taught her the life-changing principles
she now shares with all the suffering people God
has sent her way.

My mother met an old friend in the grocery store
one day who commented, "Did you know that I
am 93 years old?"

Mother asked, "What's it like to be 93?"

The beautiful reply came, "To be 93, you can't be a sissy!"

Why is God sometimes silent? His silence does not mean He is absent. In John 14:16 He promised us a Helper, "that He may abide with you forever" (KJV). In Matthew 28:20 He promised to be with us always, even to the end of the age. God is in the middle of the crisis proving His faithfulness when what we really want from Him are immediate results.

Often God seems to remain silent in the area of morality. Have you ever wondered why God lets evil people get ahead and allows the poor to be crushed? From the sidelines we are often tempted to urge, "God, do something!" Sometimes we feel like Elijah at Horeb (1 Kings 19:14) when he confronted God: "Lord, I am the only decent person left. Everyone else has turned to evil. I am the only one who cares." Have you ever felt like that?

Hosea can also tell us about the cost of immorality. Hosea loved his wife but saw her wander away. She grew coarse and cheap and spent nights away from home with different lovers. Finally she was sold into slavery as a common prostitute. Hosea went to the slave market and bought her back because he loved her.

Like a Father

We see the heart of God in Hosea's actions. To understand God's silence, Jesus tells us that God is like a father. We must understand His nature. What is a father like? How does he help his children develop maturity?

Several years ago, when my oldest son was four or five years old, we visited friends who had a large wooded area behind their home. Every time Ed wandered off into the woods, Jo Beth would tell me, "Go get him!"

I brought him back again and again, "Ed, stay here! Don't go into the woods!"

But he forgot my firm order and mean look. I decided that if he wandered off again, I would let him go. In a few minutes he was gone again. As he walked deeper and deeper into the woods, I hid behind the trees, but stayed nearby. I watched him go down the strange trails and occasionally turn around. He couldn't see me. He just kept trudging ahead as he walked on and on. Suddenly he stopped. Waves of panic came over him. As he began to cry, I stepped out from behind a tree and said, "Son, are you ready to go home?"

He looked up at me and said simply, "Ed's lost!"

God is like a father. Where do you think the Father is when we start down dead-end streets or wander into the black forests of sin and rebellion? At any moment He could step out, block our path, and say, "Don't do that. That is wrong. That will cause you problems!" Or He could come out and say, "Oh, I will take care of that pain. Don't worry about it. It will go away." Or He might say, "I see you grappling with that question and that decision. Here is my answer for you."

Because God is like a father who loves, He lets us walk as free moral agents and not as puppets on a string. He allows us to wander until we finally admit, "Lord, I am lost and cannot go on by myself." Then the Father takes us back to His house, and we discover that His door has been open all the time, just waiting for us to come inside.

The problem in Job's circumstances was not the absence or the silence of God. The real problem was Job's cold heart! "Oh that I knew where I might find Him!" he cries (23:3 NASB). If that is your cry, take just one step toward God and He will come out from behind that tree. He will even do more than point you toward home; He will carry you all the way. He will take you back home to Himself.

Chapter Insights

1. God's timetable should not be misinterpreted as His silence.
2. Sometimes we accuse God of silence because He chooses not to repeat Himself.
3. If we use crucial situations of tragedy and pain as times to trust in the Lord completely, He will give us strength and insight beyond our dreams.

9

Living Yesterday Today

*[God] said to man, "The fear of the Lord—
that is wisdom, and to shun evil is understanding"
(Job 28:28).*

*How I long for the months gone by, for the days
when God watched over me! (Job 29:2).*

• • • • •

There are two kinds of speakers—those who
have something to say, and those who have to say
something. Job's friends are in the latter category.
Chapter after chapter, verse after verse, they
continue to challenge, philosophize, and indict.
They even throw in a little theology.

Job answers Bildad specifically in chapter 26.
Then in chapters 27 through 31 Job pours out his
final soliloquy on his innocence. Chapter 28 is
profound on the lifelong search for wisdom and
understanding. The authors of Job (28:28) and
Proverbs (1:7) both agree that the fear of the Lord

is the beginning of wisdom. In the first 11 verses of Job 28, Job uses a mining metaphor and compares the search for wisdom with the search for precious minerals. His description of the mining process is surprisingly up-to-date. In verses 12-19 Job speaks of the value of wisdom and places it far above that of all the precious jewels and metals which were prized in his day.

What is wisdom? Some define it as applied knowledge. That definition does not go far enough. Knowledge without moral content is a dangerous thing! A Swedish astrophysicist has said the first verse in the Bible should read, "In the beginning was an original cloud, magnetized, perhaps a light-year, or 6 trillion miles, in its diameter." That sounds rather impressive. However, the learned professor should answer two questions: First, "What was that cloud made of?" Second, "Who put it there?" Job maintained that a man begins to understand something about the mysteries of life when he stands before God in awe, reverence, and obedience to worship Him. "The fear of the Lord is the beginning of wisdom, and knowledge of the Holy One is understanding" (Proverbs 9:10). We can know facts, but only God can give wisdom. The first step toward wisdom is obedience, and Job recognized this fact: "Behold, the fear of the Lord, that is wisdom" (28:28 NASB).

Yesterday's Security

In chapters 29 through 31 Job longs for his glorious past. In 29:2 he weeps, "How I long for the months gone by, for the days when God watched over me!'' He recalls his past life of riches and good health, when his children were alive and he had prestige among his peers. We are skilled at taking backward looks. A few moments of introspection and we become authorities on yesterday! The study and interpretation of history is very important, but we must not live in the past!

For some people there is a need to return to a security we once knew. For others it is a return to a time of no responsibility. We may recall the early days of our family and career, when we could make a decision and it would not matter whether it was right or wrong. We remember years in the military, when there was always someone higher up to answer the hard questions. At one time we could put our minds into neutral and go where we were pushed. But times have changed!

Others live in the past because it was so very beautiful. Usually our memory has played tricks on us, and we become like the Israelites in the wilderness who longed for the leeks and the garlic of Egypt. They had forgotten about slavery, bricks without straw, and life under the Egyptian lash. While in the wilderness, they continually accused Moses of depriving them of ''the good old days.'' They were so busy looking back that they lived in the present with a false, idealized view of the past. Notice something: Not a single one of those backward looking Israelites entered the Promised Land!

After I had been away from my boyhood home for several years, I decided to take my oldest son, Ed, to see the place where I had grown up. I especially wanted to show him the big tree I had climbed as a boy. He had heard all the stories about that important tree. When we came to the tree I said, "Son, there it is. That's the tree I've told you so much about."

"You mean that's the big tree?"

"Yes. That's the one."

"That's the one you fell out of?"

"Yes."

"That's the tree where you made the swing and had your tree house?"

"Yes."

Ed was not impressed! Although we were standing before a scrubby little tree barely more than 10 or 12 feet high, I had remembered a spectacular tree. Surely we were looking at a miracle: Over the years that tree had shrunk!

Isn't that the way it always is? We go back to our hometown and see that things are totally different from our memories. The people are not quite as friendly; the houses are smaller; the grass is not as green as we remembered. We can romanticize the past, but when we go back, yesterday is gone forever!

Still others want to go back in time to change things or to fix things. They would make other decisions; they would patch up that relationship; they would mend that heartbreak. They are like Esau, who sobbed over his past with tears that were too late! He had sold his birthright for a bowl of soup, and all the treasure of the world could not buy it back.

Hell in the Present Tense

Some want to go back for the same reason Job

did: The present was a hell on earth! He had lost everything of human worth and value; physical and mental anguish tormented him. He wanted to go back! We can understand that.

Let us face reality: The calories we burn trying to turn back the calendar, lamenting over what used to be or might have been, become an exercise in futility. The past is over! Learn from it, but don't dwell on it.

If we accept temptation, suffering, old age, and death as part of God's whole gift of life, we can take the worst of experiences. Then, by God's grace and in His economy, they are used by Him for our good and for His glory. This is what Job was trying to comprehend.

We have an advantage over Job. While he grappled with suffering and his search for wisdom, he did not have the secret that Paul gave us: "Forgetting what is behind and straining toward what is ahead, I press on toward the goal to win the prize for which God has called me heavenward in Christ Jesus" (Philippians 3:13,14). Forget those things which are behind. Put them in the past!

Plan Ahead

Goals and dreams are vital ingredients in any life. Without them we are in serious emotional and spiritual trouble. A tremendous little book entitled *The One-Minute Manager*, written by Blanchard and Johnson, describes goal-setting. The authors maintain that the problem with corporations and individuals is that they do not set goals and then plan strategies to accomplish those goals.

The writers explain that for most people, operating in their vocation is like bowling with a sheet hanging in front of the pins. The "bowler" gets behind the line and rolls the bowling ball down the lane. He hears a crash from behind the sheet, but he doesn't know what was accomplished. Someone asks, "How did you do?" He responds, "I don't really know, but it felt good. I can't see, but it sounded like I made a pretty good shot!" The authors say this is the way some people live. Nebulous goals can be frustrating and unsatisfying at best.

Would it make sense to play golf at night? Of course not! Why? Because you can't see the greens; you can't tell how you are doing. Imagine a football game with no goal lines: No goal lines, no game! And yet this is exactly the way many people operate their lives and their vocations. We cannot take for granted that those who work with us know what to do and where they're going. Each person must have specific goals.

Job has no goals. He laments his losses: his wealth, his health, his children, his prestige. He spends so much time in the past that he forgets about the treasure he still possesses.

Having It All!

Job still has God! If a man has everything in this life but is without God, he really has nothing at all. If he loses everything in this life but still has God, he has it all! This is not a riddle; it is actually true. Job finally discovers that through suffering and hardship he has learned lessons which otherwise he would have missed. He becomes a different person!

Many times we hear people who have endured trauma say, "I would not go through that valley again for anything in the world, but neither would I have *missed* going through it for anything in the world." The crisis became the decisive event of their life.

Suffering is productive. In Romans 5:3 Paul says that we are to rejoice in our suffering. James talks about rejoicing when we encounter trials (1:2). The book of Hebrews has another word about rejoicing under the discipline of God (12:10,11). In the Sermon on the Mount, Jesus told us to rejoice.

Does this mean that when I am struggling with the shadow of death, or I have an overwhelming health or emotional problem, I am to rejoice in it? Not at all! We are not to rejoice in the suffering itself. That would be masochistic. We are not expected to enjoy pain. Only neurotics enjoy having something wrong with them! Scripture does not exalt that kind of morbidity.

Instead, we are to rejoice in our suffering because of our confidence that God is at work producing something of significance. It is almost like the pain that accompanies childbirth. A mother cries, "I cannot stand this pain!" Indeed, she could not except for the knowledge that through such pain her child will be born. Her pain is leading to something beautiful and wonderful and miraculous! Suffering comes, and we live through it. We ask "Why?" and we even shake our fist at God, as Job did. Through it all, though, we can know that God is in charge; He is teaching us; He is producing something in our lives that could never be there if we did not suffer.

From Suffering to Hope

Paul describes the progressive stages we go through when we suffer: "We also rejoice in our sufferings, because we know that suffering produces perseverance; perseverance, character; and character, hope" (Romans 5:3,4). A better translation for perseverance would be "steadiness." Suffering produces *steadiness*. The Greek literally says that suffering helps us to stand up under pressure. It is the pressure and push of the agonizing moment that helps us. Have you ever seen someone put a saddle on a horse for the first time? Horses respond in different ways. Some panic: Their nostrils flare; their eyes roll back; they buck; they kick. Others stand trembling, and sometimes go into shock. People react to suffering in much the same way. However, if we endure, if we glory in it, that suffering produces steadiness.

Have you ever had something knock you off your feet, but somehow you managed to survive it? Then something else comes along that is equally traumatic, and you respond with a steadiness in this new situation that you never even knew you had. The pressure can be intense, but you are steady because of your previous experiences.

Consider the next step. Paul says, "Suffering produces character." You do not go berserk or misinterpret a situation, as you once did, because now your character has been developed. The word "character" literally means, "You have been tested." In television commercials, steel-belted radial tires are shown being subjected to potholes, hot desert sand, bumpy railroads, and even boards with huge nails. Then the commercial zooms in for a close-up of that tire. It looks like it has just been taken from the shelf of a retail store! That is the picture portrayed by this Greek word for "character."

The teacher asked Mary what she wanted to be when she grew up. Without a pause the little girl replied, "A returned missionary!" Think about it: That honest desire holds a world of truth! She wanted the reward without leaving home, without the pain of separation and change.

God wants to make veterans out of all of us. In order to do that, He knows that we must experience different degrees of suffering. He has promised that He will not give us anything to face without also providing sufficient strength to stand up under it, to live with it, or to live through it. We need to remember that privation and suffering are the means of producing steadiness and character.

Next, Paul says that suffering also produces hope. This "hope" is not just pie-in-the-sky wishful thinking. Instead, it is the confidence that allows us to say, "I am better than I used to be. There is a quietness within me." This same hope reassures us that we are growing in grace to become like Jesus Christ.

It is because of the hope we have as Christians that we can live through the pain of suffering,

privation, and heartache; through times of broken-
ness, when our lives are shattered and our dreams
are destroyed. This hope is confidence in God.

Romans 5:5 teaches us one of the most important truths in the Bible: "Hope does not disappoint
us, because God has poured out his love into our
hearts by the Holy Spirit, whom he has given us."
Look what suffering and tribulation give us: His
love.

Yet suffering is painful! Sometimes we are like
the woman who was constantly complaining about
her plight. Someone said to her, "You shouldn't
complain all the time; you're a Christian." The
woman replied, "The Bible says we will go through
tribulation. I'm going through tribulation, and
God knows I have the right to 'tribulate' a little."

It is all right to "tribulate" a little! But in the
tribulation remember the end result of suffering:
It produces steadiness, and steadiness produces
character, and character produces hope, and hope
produces confidence. Confidence in what? Confidence in the day that the love of God will be
"shed abroad," filling our hearts. As we press
toward the goal, God continues to shape us into
the man or woman He intends us to be. Should
we long for "the good old days"? Not one bit!
The best is yet to be.

If suffering has come to your life, then you can
know that God will use it. We must learn, with
Paul, how to forget those things which lie behind
and to strain forward to that mark which lies
before us, pressing always toward the prize of the
high calling of God in Christ Jesus. *That* is the
secret of successful living!

Chapter Insights

1. Although we do not always feel or see God's presence, He *never* stops watching over His children.
2. The security of yesterday can keep us locked away from the promise of tomorrow.
3. Genuine faith in God is the only reason human beings have for letting go of yesterday.
4. In God's hands, our suffering is always used for His glory and our good.
5. Goals give perspective and purpose to our lives and keep us from being "stopped cold" by suffering. Suffering ultimately produces confidence in God when we trust Him completely.

10

Sense in the Middle of Nonsense

It is not only the old who are wise, nor only the aged who understand what is right. Therefore I say: Listen to me; I too will tell you what I know (Job 32:9,10).

Job has not marshaled his words against me, and I will not answer him with your arguments (Job 32:14).

● ● ● ● ●

To this point the three friends of Job—Eliphaz, Bildad, and Zophar—have really worked him over! From the start of the discussion, a large crowd of bystanders observed the debate. They have been listening to four of the most prestigious leaders in that region. Among these, Job is the most respected of all. Eventually a young fellow sticks his head up above the crowd and observes, "All of you are turkeys! Even with all your experience, none of you has any common sense."

The Generation Gap

His name is Elihu, the voice of youth. "I thought you older fellows had all the answers. If I had lived as long as you, surely I could have made some sense out of this situation. You have been trying to help Job, and he has tried to defend himself. After that, when he took the offensive, you took the other side." Elihu scoffs at the ignorance of his elders: "I thought the longer you lived, the smarter you became, but you older folks are downright stupid!" Talk about a generation gap!

We might as well be honest about it: The gap exists in every generation! During the 25,000 days of normal lifespan there will inevitably be conflict between young and old as they interact with each other. Our tastes are different. The young and the old appreciate different styles of music and of dress. There is a difference in the way we think and the way we approach life—in our vocabularies, in our mathematics, and even in our viewpoints! Elihu boldly stands up and says, "I'm a young man, but I have more sense than all the rest of you."

There is a difference between youth and old age, and Elihu realizes it. He listens as Job's three "friends" give their verbose speeches. Not only has he enjoyed about as much of it as he can stand, but he also has some opinions of his own. Read his discourse, and you will discover that his insights are far superior to those of Eliphaz, Bildad, and Zophar.

Words Without Knowledge

While Elihu has many fine qualities, he also has some glaring shortcomings. As is often the plight of the younger generation, he believes that he was born an educated person. I hate to confess this, but as a high school graduate, I thought I knew everything!

Since I was an alumnus of the *only* high school in Laurel, Mississippi, I was prepared to handle anything that life would throw at me. When I took the entrance exams at the University of Alabama, there was one part I will never forget. There was a picture of hoofs and paws and wings, and I was supposed to identify each one and say whether it was the right or left wing, the back or front hoof, and so forth. Being a country boy, I passed the test with flying colors. In fact, I did too well! I found myself in advanced algebra and trigonometry, and sophomore English. I was in over my head! After the first week I was drowning. In all my pride I discovered that there was not a more unprepared student at the University of Alabama than Edwin Young!

Elihu has not yet had such an experience. This cocky guy has enough self-confidence for his entire generation! He stands up in the middle of his elders and says, "Let me set the record straight for you!"

In Job 32:14 we find, "But Job has not marshaled his words against me, and I will not answer him with your arguments." Elihu tells them, "Job hasn't debated with me yet! He has cut all of you down, and you still haven't answered any of his arguments or solved any of his problems. You have spoken pious, pedestrian shibboleths. Job, you don't have a chance! I'm dynamite!"

Also, Elihu is harsh and overbearing; he has a mean spirit. So often, the young see only black and white—never any grays. Something is either right or wrong—period. The young are notoriously intolerant of compromise; they jump to conclusions and are dogmatic about every subject. They cannot understand how the world has gotten into such a mess!

On the other hand, Elihu does have some admirable qualities. One is his faith. As some of us get older, our faith lags behind. We accept everything because "It has always been like this. After all, what can we do about liquor or prostitution or pornography?" Elihu does not accept the older generation's view of the status quo. He says, "You are wrong! We can do something about it! We can change people and things!" In spite of Job's dilemma and the pious, insincere answers from his holier-than-thou friends, Elihu sees some answers. He believes that God is in the midst of Job's troubles. He has faith—but not enough faith!

He volunteers to get involved. He sacrifices himself on the altar of inexperience, but he is available! Another quality of Elihu is that he knows when to get angry. It is very important to know when to get angry. There's something wrong with a Christian who never gets angry. We must learn how to handle anger when it occurs.

We usually get angry when people offend or attack us. Not Elihu! He gets angry because the principle of Bildad's argument is wrong. Bildad tells Job that he has not suffered enough: "Job, you don't understand life. God should make you suffer more!"

But Elihu, with all his faults, uses his faith on Job's behalf. He knows how to handle anger, and he knows how to help Job find solutions to his problems. Job's other friends are deadlocked. They have exhausted their resources; they have no more ammunition.

It is important that we go beyond the Old Testament view of age versus youth and look at the New Testament as well. The Old Testament pictures the superiority of old age and the inferiority of youth. In the New Testament we find a blending of the young and old. Paul advised young Timothy, "Don't let the world despise your youth" (1 Timothy 4:12). The young and old were all together at Pentecost. In his letters, Paul noted the unity between Jew and Gentile, bond and free, young and old, and male and female because Jesus has broken down the walls of partition.

Young men see visions; old men dream dreams. A church needs both: dreams and visions, young and old. The mix assures a strong, mature body of Christ.

Saved Alone

A businessman lost everything he had in the great Chicago fire. Since this took place before the days of insurance coverage, he was forced to turn to some friends for help. Penniless, he borrowed money to send his wife and children to Europe while he tried to reconstruct his business and home. As his wife and two children were crossing the ocean, a great storm destroyed their ship. As a rescue ship approached, that mother held her two babies above the waves. Suddenly a powerful wave ripped both children from her arms and plunged them into the raging sea. She was saved, but her children were lost.

When she reached port, she cabled her husband "SAVED ALONE." When that man learned of this further tragedy, he felt like a modern Job. For weeks he was afraid to touch a gun or a knife or go to a high place for fear that he might take his own life. Then something miraculous happened! As he prayed the heavens opened, and God exploded into his life and heart. That man discovered what so many of us have learned in times of suffering and death: "My grace is sufficient." In that moment of assurance he picked up a pen and wrote these words:

> When peace like a river attendeth my way
> When sorrows like sea billows roll,
> Whatever my lot, Thou hast taught me
>   to say,
> "It is well, it is well with my soul!"

Chapter Insights

1. Young people need to be heard for the freshness and creativity they can offer to a stale or obsolete perspective.
2. Anger at principles rather than persons should be the Christian's approach.
3. Complete confidence in the Lord Jesus Christ gives a person the resources from within to turn any tragedy into victory.

11

Whatever Happened to Sin?

His anger never punishes and he does not take the least notice of wickedness (Job 35:15).

The Lord answered Job out of the storm. He said:

"Who is this that darkens my counsel with words without knowledge? Brace yourself like a man; I will question you, and you shall answer me. Where were you when I laid the earth's foundation? Tell me, if you understand. Who marked off its dimensions? Surely you know! Who stretched a measuring line across it? On what were its footings set, or who laid its cornerstone—while the morning stars sang together and all the angels shouted for joy?" (Job 38:1-7).

I know that you can do all things; no plan of yours can be thwarted. You asked, "Who is this that obscures my counsel without knowledge?" Surely I spoke of things I did not understand, things too wonderful for me to know. You said, "Listen now, and I will speak; I will question you,

*and you shall answer me." My ears had heard of
you but now my eyes have seen you (Job 42:2-5).*

*After Job had prayed for his friends, the Lord
made him prosperous again and gave him twice
as much as he had before (Job 42:10).*

● ● ● ● ●

One version of Job 35:15 states, "God is not
serious about sin."

"God is not serious about sin." Do you believe
that? Karl Menninger, a leading psychotherapist,
has written a book entitled *Whatever Happened
to Sin?* His thesis is that in our modern civilization we have explained away guilt and sin and
wrongdoing. We have said that it doesn't exist
anymore. "But," says the doctor, "sin is real!"
Menninger states that we need a fresh understanding of old-fashioned biblical sin and forgiveness.

Elihu says, "God doesn't take sin seriously. He
is not interested in the affairs of humans!"

Does God care about how a person lives? Does
your sin harm God? If you're terrible, you're terrible. If you're good, you're good. Why should
God care? This is the concept that Elihu, the young
counselor, develops. God is not seriously concerned about sin.

The devil told Eve in the Garden of Eden
exactly the same thing: "If you eat of that fruit
you will be wise, you will be free, you will have
a new zest in life." The biggest lie of all is that
God does not care about your sin, that it makes
no difference to God about how you live or what
you do.

Sin is beguiling, appealing, alluring. It is magnetic. It seems to hold tremendous promise. Not by accident, a best-selling perfume years ago was called "My Sin." The inference was that this perfume would cause a bewitching glamour and that the wearer would have men falling at her feet! In fantasy, sin always seems to be beautiful and alluring. In reality, it is exactly the opposite.

Elihu's advice is as useless to Job as the counsel of the three friends. They all accuse Job of being a big hypocrite. All have the same theological concept, although they approach the problem from different perspectives. All accuse: "Job, you're a rascal. You have fooled everyone. We know you're a rascal, God knows you're a rascal, and you're being justly punished for what you have done. Confess your sin!"

From Job 26 to 31 Job defends himself by telling everyone how wonderful he really is. Chapter 29 voices the epitome of ego. Job boasts, "I help the blind. I help the lame. I help the deaf. I help the widows. I participate in civic causes. I feed the poor." In chapter 29 he uses the word "I" over 50 times. In chapters 30 and 31 he uses that personal pronoun over 100 times!

Job's problem is becoming obvious. He has "I" trouble. His sin is not at all the sin his three friends have stated. Job's sin could never be revealed apart from such a time of trouble. Only at this time, when he is naked and impoverished, with his health broken and his family rejecting him, are we able to see Job's sin. God knows Job's problem all along; He had diagnosed the "heart trouble" in the days of Noah: "For the intent of man's heart is evil from his youth!'' (Genesis 8:21 NASB). Job's friends look on his outward appearance (as does Satan), but God looks in his heart. Surely the Lord had blessed Job with abundant good fortune in his former years. In addition to wealth and children, he had prestige: counsel for every situation and an opinion on every subject. God knows that ''His man Job'' has enough ''stuff'' to outlast Satan's attack and that during this time of tribulation he can learn about humility and about righteousness (Ezekiel 14:14,20).

In chapters 32 through 37 we find a long account by this young unknown theologian, Elihu. He makes more sense than Job's three older friends— as far as he goes with his remarks. Elihu falsely believes that God is not concerned about our sin. Other than this, much of what Elihu says is true. He counsels, ''Job, your arms are too short to box with God. You are under the sovereignty of God. He is running this whole universe. Therefore, for you to try to bring your case before a court of justice is a waste of time.

''But,'' Elihu says, ''by the same token, God is not serious about sin.'' Elihu has a word of truth about the sovereignty of God, but dangerously false words concerning sin.

Does God take sin seriously? Many people would say, ''Yes, He does.'' Yet in their conduct they do not live as though they truly believe it.

What Exactly Is Sin?

Sin is breaking the law, according to 1 John 3:4; it is doing something that is wrong. Sin also is not doing something that is right! When the priest and the Levite found the Samaritan beaten and robbed by the road, they did not search him to see if the robbers had missed some pennies in his pockets. Instead, their sin was the sin of *omission*. It is what they did *not* do that was evil. In the last judgment, a whole group of individuals will be condemned to outer darkness. Why? Because of something they did? No! They will be condemned because of what they did *not* do! They did not meet God through His Son, Jesus Christ. Sin is not only doing wrong; it is also *not* doing what is right when we have the opportunity to do it. If we live among people who are suffering and dying, and we do not bother to get involved, that is sin—the sin of *omission*.

But the supreme sin is neither doing wrong nor refusing to do what is right; it is not *being* right! "As many as received Him, to them gave He power to *become* the sons of God" (John 1:12 KJV). Becoming a Christian is *right being*. When we refuse to be a son or a daughter of God, when we refuse to be adopted into the family of God through Jesus Christ, we have committed the supreme sin. Sin is the refusal to be right with God through Christ.

Now we see why God, like a father, takes sin seriously, whatever its form. At the beginning of Job's story, we see him as a family man who is so meticulous in "right doing" that he offers sacrifices for his children just in case they had committed an unknown sin! (1:5). Later Job has the idea, "It does not make any difference whether you do right or wrong. God is not concerned.

Therefore, being good does not help. Evil does not make any difference. You might as well go right down the middle and compromise" (chapter 21).

Job's Final Lament

Through all these chapters, Job voices one theme: "Oh, that I knew where I might find Him! Please, God, show up on this awful scene. Let me know You're there!" Job has been lashing out, crying in confusion. He is saying many contradictory things now. Perhaps he is not really aware of all he is saying. His many words cry out, "I just want to find God. Step up, God, and be counted."

By this time the three friends are exhausted. Job has said everything a suffering, discredited, disenfranchised individual can say. The young theologue, Elihu, has thrown in his comments, better than anything said previously, but still not totally on target. Then God speaks: "Then the Lord answered Job out of the storm" (Job 38:1).

When God Speaks

What would we expect God to say to Job in the middle of his suffering? It would seem logical for God to say, "Job, you don't know what is going on. There is a football game going on between Myself and the devil. Job, your problem is simple; you are the football!" He might say, "Job, you are learning some tremendous things through your suffering." That is true: Suffering develops character. Suffering also provides an example for other people. Suffering also reveals hidden sin. All of these factors are involved in Job's case.

God might offer hope to Job. Perhaps He will answer the accusations that Job has brought against Him. Job has said, "God is insensitive. He does not care. He is aloof." He has said, "God, You are all-powerful, but You have no heart." He has challenged the love of God; he has questioned His character!

Job's faith is not truly in God. It is much like the faith of so many of us. When calamity comes, we cry, "Oh, God, why has all this happened to me? I am losing my faith." Such a statement reveals that our faith has not truly been in God. Instead, it has been in what God could do for us! When we suffer the loss of God's *help*, we say we are losing our faith. In reality, our faith has been in our well-being. If our faith were truly in God, we could lose everything else and still have faith. When our faith is in our own well-being, we cry, "Oh, God, don't You care? I am losing my belief in You."

We might expect God to point this out to Job in His address. That would be profound! But God does not mention any of these answers. God's reply to Job comes in chapter 38, and what a reply it is! *God presents a lecture on nature appreciation!* This address would be appreciated greatly by the Audubon Society. Friends of the Earth would be overwhelmed! But is it appropriate to deliver it to *Job?* Job wants hard answers. "Identify with me; walk in my shoes. I have been smashed in every area of life!" When God speaks to this dying man out of the storm, He gives a *nature lesson*! In Job 38:2,3 God says, "Job, stand up! I know you are hurting, but stand up and get ready to move fast! You have been questioning me and slandering me. First you answer *My* questions, then I will answer *your* questions, and then we will have this whole matter worked out!"

God then asks His first question.

> Where were you when I laid the foundations of the earth? Tell me, if you know so much. Do you know how its dimensions were determined, and who did the surveying? What supports its foundations, and who laid its cornerstone, as the morning stars sang together and all the angels shouted for joy? (38:4-7 TLB).

What is holding this earth up? Nobody really knows. God asks, "Job, do *you* know? Were you there when the earth was flung into space?"

These four chapters contain the longest word of teaching directly from the mouth of God in all of Scripture. He talks about the sunrise in 38:12:

> Have you ever once commanded the morning to appear, and caused the dawn to rise in the east? (TLB).

In 38:22 He asks:

> Have you visited the treasuries of the snow, or seen where hail is made and stored? (TLB).

In 38:25-27 He talks about thunderstorms:

> Who dug the valleys for the torrents of rain? Who laid out the path for the lightning,

causing the rain to fall upon the barren deserts, so that the parched and barren ground is satisfied with water, and tender grass springs up? (TLB).

In 38:39,40 He talks about the lioness:

Can you stalk prey like a lioness, to satisfy the young lions' appetites as they lie in their dens, or lie in wait in the jungle? (TLB).

God asks about mountain goats in 39:1:

Do you know how mountain goats give birth? Have you ever seen them giving birth to their young? (TLB).

In 39:5,6 He talks about wild donkeys:

Who makes the wild donkeys wild? I have placed them in the wilderness and given them salt plains to live in (TLB).

In 39:16-18 He asks about the ostrich:

She ignores her young as though they weren't her own, and is unconcerned though they die, for God has deprived her of wisdom. But whenever she jumps up to run, she passes the swiftest horse with its rider (TLB).

In 39:19 God asks:

Have you given the horse strength, or clothed his neck with a quivering mane? (TLB).

The Lord goes on, asking about an elephant, a crocodile, all kinds of eagles and birds and ravens—all of nature! He speaks of such things to a man who is frustrated, bitter, and angry. What is God's purpose? He is simply asking Job in the midst of his arrogance, "Where were you, Job, when all these things took place?"

When we face suffering, we should pick up our Bibles and read Job 38-41. Prayerfully, we can ask, "Oh, God, what do You have to say to me about all this?" In these chapters God shows how we are to think when suffering comes. There are no complicated riddles here, no theological problems. Are you depressed? Embittered? Rejected? Sick? Worried? Confused? Mentally disturbed? Are you going through a domestic crisis? Does your child have problems that you cannnot solve? You are crying out, "I am suffering beyond my capacity to bear!" Pick up your Bible and read what God said to Job. Through it He will speak to you.

God asks in 40:2, "Do you still want to argue with the Almighty, or will you yield? Do you, God's critic, have the answers?" In the middle of this nature lecture Job makes one brief comment. It takes him three chapters to clear his throat!

Job has been looking for a showdown. He has said, "Oh, God, I wish I could bring You into court. Oh, God, I wish You had some answers for me. God, step forward; I want to deal with You. Why are the heavens made of brass?" We have all said such words in our pain: "Come on, God. I am ready for You!" When God does come, and asks Job for some initial response, all the patriarch can do is stammer and stutter, "I am nothing; how could I ever find the answers? I lay my hand upon my mouth in silence. I have said too much already."

God continued with His nature lecture. We get

to Job's reply in 42:2,3: "I know that you can do anything and that no one can stop you. You ask who it is who has so foolishly denied your providence. It is I. I was talking about things I know nothing about and did not understand, things far too wonderful for me" (TLB). Job then quotes back to God what He said at the beginning of His discourse: "Listen and I will speak! Let me put the questions to you! See if you can answer them!" (42:4 TLB). Job now answers in 42:5, "I had heard about you before, but now I have seen you, and I loathe myself and repent in dust and ashes" (TLB). Most translations say, "I abhor myself and repent in dust and ashes." When Job is confronted by God, he conducts himself like every other biblical person when confronted directly by God: With fear and trembling he falls flat on his face and becomes silent!

What a response! We need to understand this, for it is a most profound truth to learn!

Many people talk about having visions of God or of seeing Jesus as though He were a big statue. They comment, "How wonderful it was to be in the presence of God! How marvelous it was! I wanted to stay there and praise Him and love Him. I came away shouting and laughing." There is not a single example of such an encounter with God in the entire Bible. Without a single exception, when Scripture describes a person's encounter with God, that person is humbled and broken by the experience. He responds exactly as did Job, who said, "I abhor myself!" Job repented in dust and ashes. He fell flat on his face and kept his mouth shut. (Compare Isaiah's response in Isaiah 6:5.)

That is where repentance begins. The old Puritans prayed, "Oh, God, give me tears of repentance." Job falls prostrate before the Lord. Consider the meaning of his words "I abhor myself." The word "abhor" means, in Hebrew, "Something that just melts away." There is an important lesson to be learned from this expression.

How do we deal with sin today? We deal with it humanly. We evaluate our character problems such as bitterness, temper, and immorality. We then say with great determination and willpower, "I am going to correct this." Our plan for improvement includes purchasing as many books and attending as many seminars as we can on self-improvement. We begin the process of "re-forming" ourselves much the way we would break a large chunk of ice...hammer away!

God is not impressed by our reforming. There is not a word in the Bible about straightening out our problem areas. The Bible never mentions trying to do better. It never recommends "Giving it all you have to give." Instead, the Bible talks about *repentance*! God does not want us to *get* better; He wants us to *be* better, and that must begin with repentance. We step out into the sun. Our sin is not just beaten down, shattered like broken ice; it is melted away as we lie flat on our faces with our mouth shut, broken before God.

Job's Great Awakening

God never leaves any loose ends when He deals with a situation. There are some final details to be carefully observed before this book is laid aside. Job has experienced the absence of God and the absence of all human comfort. He has experienced agonizing pain across the months or possibly years, suffering with a disease like elephantiasis. He is a totally discredited, slandered man, without any recourse, without any hope, in abject depression. Then Job comes to final conclusions, which will carry him through all crisis moments for the rest of his life. The man of suffering says, "God, You are running this universe. You are in control. I do not understand it. I do not *have* to understand it. I only know that You are in control. I realize that my problem has been one of self-righteousness."

Job said in effect, in 29:14, "I clothe myself with righteousness." We also do that—until God comes near! Then we must cry out, as do Amos and Isaiah and Job and the publican, "Oh God, be merciful to me, a sinner." Job yields: "I retract and I repent!" Why? Previously Job has known *about* God; now he knows God *personally*!

God then turns to the three friends—Eliphaz, Bildad, and Zophar (42:7). In so many words, God says to them, "Job's problem has been one of self-righteousness. You never even touched upon that truth in all your condemnation of Job. You missed the whole point of his suffering! Your major problem is your theology. It is so hard and so cold that you forget about the needs of people."

The problem with these three friends is that they never pray; they never ask God what they should say to Job. Not once do they volunteer to say a prayer for Job. They have all the answers; their closed theology makes any further revelation from God impossible.

God says, "You must do some sacrificing, Eliphaz, Bildad, and Zophar!" He tells them what sacrifices He requires. It is important to recognize that the number of these sacrifices is much greater than those required for only three people. God asks them for enough rams and oxen to pay for the sins of an entire nation on the Day of Atonement! In the eyes of God, their sin is enormous!

However, even all these sacrifices are not sufficient for the atonement of these ancient Pharisees. God says, "If Job will pray for you, I will totally forgive your sin against him." God stresses the important dimension of prayer! To the three friends He says, "Unless Job prays for you, you will have to live with your sin. Apart from his prayer for you, I will not forgive you."

James wrote, "Ye have not because ye ask not" (James 4:2 KJV). How much more we could have if we prayed for other people! How much more God would do in other people's lives if we would intercede for them! God wants to give to us, to bless us, to fill us, to nourish us, to use us, if only we would pray for each other. We have not because we ask not! Job is called upon to be an intercessor for these three friends who have rudely kicked him at the lowest moment of his life.

After such treatment, would *you* have prayed for them? Think about someone you do not like, someone who has really abused you, who had a chance to say a good word for you but did not do it. Think of someone who has slandered you, has let you down, has disappointed you, has abused you, has belittled you. Think of the grudge you carry toward that person. Here is a chance for you to get even: Refuse to pray for that person!

These three friends have lacerated Job publicly and now their restoration with God and their sanity for the rest of their lives depends on Job's praying for them! What would you have done?

Here we see Job as the intercessor. Perhaps his prayer goes something like this: "Lord, You know my three friends. They have been cold and hard and deceitful. But, Lord, I was the same way. You have forgiven me. Please forgive them. Lord, my three friends have been so insensitive and so tough on me, and they really hurt me. But, Lord, I have done worse than they. I have slandered You, and You have forgiven me. Please, Lord, forgive them."

In James 5:16 there is an interesting statement: "Confess your sins to one another, and pray for one another, so that you may be healed" (NASB). Was Job's prayer necessary also for his own complete forgiveness? Was it a sign of his true repentance? "And the Lord restored the fortunes of Job when he prayed for his friends" (42:10 NASB). After Job prayed for his friends, the Lord makes him prosperous again and gives him twice as much as he had before. Not only is Job forgiven, but God *doubles* his blessings! Next, his family comes to see him. They throw a big party for Job, and all of them bring gifts as tokens of their love and their esteem. Now they understand what has been happening to him!

Perhaps this is the first time that Job has ever truly enjoyed his friends. Before he had been the superior man; he had given, helped, and counseled from a position of aloofness. Now he has had to receive from others, and it is much more difficult to receive than it is to give! It changes the character of a man. God has broken all the pride and self-righteousness within his man, Job.

In 1 Peter 4 the writer tells us that after someone has suffered, you can count on him. He is like broken bread and poured-out wine. He will take time for you. But if someone has never suffered, he may have time for you only if you are talking about what interests him. Job now has time for his friends. He listens. He cries. He takes a back seat, and God gives him extras because Job knows that true treasure is not of this world. His treasure is God!

Do you know that *your only treasure* is God Almighty? If you do, you will always have answers in a sea of trouble. All meaningful life is built upon that truth and all other possessions are absurdities! Only God is valuable. When you recognize this truth and commit your life to Jesus alone, you become a child of God, and all that belongs to Him is yours as well!

Chapter Insights

1. An understanding of sin is a prerequisite for avoiding it.
2. God's creativity and omnipotence should be sufficient evidence that God cares about all that happens to us, just as He did to Job.
3. Prayer is necessary to remind a person of his

dependence on God and of God's sufficiency for all his needs.
4. Honest prayer for a person who has offended you indicates an attitude of forgiveness.
5. Lessons are learned through suffering that could not be learned in any other way.
6. An encounter with God is a life-changing experience—every time!